Bums on Seats

Francesca Moi & Natasa Denman

First published by Busybird Publishing 2016
Copyright © 2016 Natasa Denman, Francesca Moi

ISBN:
978-0-9945839-1-8 (Print)
978-0-9945839-2-5 (Ebook)

Cover image: Kev Howlett, Busybird Publishing
Cover design: Busybird Publishing
Layout and typesetting: Busybird Publishing
Editor: Blaise van Hecke

Busybird Publishing
PO Box 855
Eltham Victoria
Australia 3095
www.busybird.com.au

Testimonials

What a team! The inexplicable dynamics of this duo is something to behold. My life, my business, my general being has improved astronomically by being in the room with these two.

James Bomford

CEO and Author, Right Click IT

I've grown both personally and professionally since working with Natasa and Francesca. Their combination of energy, passion and knowledge is infectious and supportive. I can't wait to see where I'm at in 12 months time!

Andrea Dix

Iron Butterfly

Francesca and Natasa are what you would call a match made in heaven and together they are going to make a huge impact on the success of countless individuals and businesses. I have never met anyone else with such authenticity that provides the value that these two women do with what they offer and I can't wait to benefit from their powerful collaboration. They stand out from the rest and if you want to learn how to as well then you can't afford to miss out on their combined experience, knowledge and contagious energy!

Janja Bojanic

Founder of Business Jumpstart Meetup

I've known Francesca for 12 months and her infectious personality and wisdom has kept me on the path I'm meant to be on, despite my fears trying to deter me.

Doing her Follow Me workshop started something I wasn't prepared for, the journey has been one of non-stop expansion for myself and my business since. Through our friendship I met Natasa. I wasn't sure I was ready to write my book, however the real, belief and emotional support Natasa brings to her work is rare in our online/marketing world.

The thought of these 2 collaborating gives me goose bumps. Lives WILL be changed! If you're looking for answers, these ladies have them in truckloads. Their energy will motivate, their knowledge will blow you away and their hearts will leave you feeling fuzzy and full of self-belief that you WILL take action and create magic for yourself.

Mell Balment, Founder of Dating with Kizmet
Author of What Women Really Want

Natasa and Francesca have been a rare find for me as the founder of Core Freedom. I have been running my 3 businesses as a solo business owner over 20 years but not really living the Entrepreneur part till I met Nat and the Boom girl!

They are fresh, real, fun, genuine, and loaded with practical and successful steps and tools. They walk the talk and model heart-centred business with feet firmly planted.

Anita Bentata,
Author, speaker, DV specialist, educator, psychotherapist

I've been a management consultant, author and lecturer for over 30 years and I continually seek coaching, advice and development from people who are where I'd like to move to next as I've changed business focus. Both Natasa and Francesca have helped me to accelerate turning my IP into books, events, and programs.

For me, the fun factor has to be there as well and it was! Super amazing women with great success and done in very simple, no nonsense, relational way. They are my two main 'go-to' people for my business and the real deal with loads of success behind them to prove it. I love their energy, passion and genuineness. You can't help but be motivated, excited and encouraged when you are around them – on and off line!

Linda Chaousis

Author, Speaker, Teacher, Mentor Linda Chaousis International

Natasa and Francesca are a passionate, fun loving, heart-centred; inspiring entrepreneurial pair I have ever had the pleasure of connecting with.

I knew of Natasa long before I began attending her events. Most recently joining up to B.O.S. Mastermind. The abundance of knowledge, resources, value and support has been incredible. I attended Francesca's half-day workshop as a result of hearing so much about 'the Meet-Up Queen' on Facebook and I was blown away by her drive and willingness to give so much to all. Both Natasa and Francesca give all they have learned and mastered to assist others. They don't hold anything back. Their success speaks for itself. I can't speak highly enough of these two amazing woman. Individually they are incredible, together they are a powerful force.

Anna Petrarca

Leader, mentor, Educator & Coach

I met Natasa and Francesca three months ago. In that time, with their direction and support, I have written one book, co-authored another, launched my own hair care range, started another company, been invited to keynote overseas and my feet haven't touched the ground yet. BOOM. They are the most inspiring, honest, motivational women I have ever had the pleasure to meet. Thank you with all my heart.

Megan Wright. IAT

Author, Trichologist, Educator, Success Coach and Motivational speaker.

Dedication

We would like to dedicate this book to all of those who are brave enough to step up and step out into the world of running and succeeding at public events.

Secondly to our followers and supporters who have helped us along on this journey and continue to add value so we can do what we do best.

Finally our deepest gratitude goes to our families who put up with our entrepreneurial bubbly spirit and all the travel that we do throughout the year. We love you very much and could not have done this without your support and understanding on what sparks us up.

Contents

The Language That Might Surprise You ...

We use a few terms all of the time and this will come through in this book. It's not rude or immature (even though it may seem that way if you don't know us). There are a few terms we use all of the time that may need to be explained before you begin. Here are the four we always use and say:

SMASH IT – go out and do it. Do your best work no matter what.

SHUTTUPP – seriously, that is so cool, I can't believe it, get out of here.

SEXY – something that will appeal to the market, great marketing copy.

BOOM! – and that's it, winner.

If you want to see these terms in action, follow us on Facebook, look up videos on our YouTube channels or simply join us at a live event ... It's so much Fun!

Introduction

Francesca's version …

*A*nd here we are Natasa Denman and I, Francesca Moi, co-writing a book … shutttuppp I can't believe it!

What I love about Natasa is the fact that she is incredibly genuine and down to earth. Natasa grew a million dollar business from home with 3 kids and a husband … this woman is a machine and I haven't met many people who can bring it like she does.

Once at a speaking gig, in a congress, to attract the attention of the public she started her speech singing the Australian National Anthem … like seriously? It was hilarious and she did get people's attention!

Natasa is one of those real European types. She is very welcoming to her home and loves running workshops and events from her beautiful home in Melbourne. I certainly feel very lucky to have had the opportunity so early in my business to collaborate with Natasa.

Since we have been collaborating a lot has changed in my business and simultaneously with our collaboration I have been implementing a lot of the strategies that you will learn in this book that took my business to well over 6 figures.

A lot of people say to Natasa and I that we are so lucky … as if we just sat down and magically filled up our events … well I can tell you there is no luck in what we have done.

There are 3 Key steps we have followed:

1. Have been consistent, and worked our butts off for a very long time, keep standing up after tough times and even when the events were not as booked up as we would have liked.

2. Both Nat and I worked a lot on our mindset, and dealt with each and every fear that came up along the path of success.

3. We have collaborated and surrounded ourselves with other people of influence.

Another common denominator of Nat and I is that we never give up and we don't take no for an answer. In the past 6 months Nat and I travelled to each others city to work together on a couple of different projects, while also running our own events.

Once we came up with an idea on a Monday … well this is how it went … we were planning the week and Nat said to me, 'What's on this Friday, Francesca?' And I said, 'The Book Launch Nat.' Nat, with a very surprised face said, 'That's at night … what have we got planned for the morning?' And I laughed and replied that no nothing was really on except preparing ourselves for our book launch with 100 plus attendees … and Natasa says super enthusiastic, 'Let's do a half-day workshop to raise more funds for our online course and the publishing of this book!'

I first thought she was joking but soon realised that she wasn't kidding and so I said, 'Yeah! Why not?'

We took a piece of paper and said, 'Ok, what are we teaching? How much are we charging?' And 10 minutes later we were promoting the workshop on all social medias … in only 4 days, and 4 fully packed days with other full on events, we managed to have 4 people LIVE and 10 people paid into Live streaming from various cities around Australia. We made an extra $1500 and counting from that strategy and have filmed half-day workshop that we can sell the footage from for a long time.

When Nat and I decide to do something we just don't give up and we make it happen!

The strongest point in our business relationship is that we truly feel like we must have been sisters in another life as we are super connected and call each other sis. Her kids and her husband Stuart also consider me part of the family and I couldn't be more proud to be the kids' aunty!

How Nat and I met

I love stories; I love knowing the real reasons why two people have met and why. So let me tell you how Nat and I met … I was running my business and I was finding that inviting people of influence as a guest speaker at my Meetups and empowering events was a genius idea, as it would bring more people to my events and it would give me a chance to start a relationship and collaboration with the guest speaker itself and it would give me the chance to be exposed to the guest speaker and show them what my events are about and what I am about because at each event I always start with an ice breaker game and my 15 minutes of magic …

In saying all this I was on the hunt for another successful business owner who had a big network and was seen as a person of influence in his/her niche … I was already a member of Ultimate Business Support Facebook Group Nat owns, and I remember seeing often this Natasa Denman lady so I decided to send her a Facebook friend request. After a few months in late July 2015, Nat sent me a Facebook message asking for the reason why I was contacting her. We started chatting and soon enough Nat told me that she was flying up the following week to the Gold Coast and we could catch up for a coffee.

Nat did her own research and noticed that I was running events and had already a big following. She knew the power of connecting with someone who has a big network. I knew how important it is to fill up your time as much as possible when you are travelling interstate so I offered Nat to speak at my event! Nat asked, 'Oh great yes, I'd love to be a speaker, when is your next event though? I am up there only for 3 days and have already other speaking gigs lined up.' And I said with confidence, 'I don't have an event planned for next week but I will organise one for you!'

Now I don't know if you have ever run an event but usually people don't pull off an event in 10 days. Usually people need 4-6 weeks to promote and organise an event to ensure it's not going to be a disaster with no one showing up. So Natasa was confused and unsure of how I was going to do this in only 10 days. I started to freak out thinking that she was going to expect over 100 people in the room, and if that was the case I wasn't going to be able to pull it off in 10 days. So I asked her, 'How many people would you like to be attending?' Nat said, 'Oh as I am already in the Gold Coast, I am happy with 10-15 people.' I was holding my breath as I was hoping on a number lower then 30. In 10 days I didn't think I would have had the time to promote that much so relieved I said, 'Oh Natasa, I will definitely get 20-25 people for you next week. How about the 4th August 2015?' Nat said, 'Great I am free that night!'

At the event we had 28 people attending, Nat and I found out that we are very similar in energy and together we ran a very fun and successful event. The attendees loved the night and from there Nat and I connected on Skype a few times to see how we could collaborate as our target market was exactly the same: Nat teaches business owners how to write a book in 48 hours and I teach business owners how to create a powerful and profitable following by starting a community (using Meetup and Facebook) BOOM … we have a joint venture and help each other promote our workshops.

The more we connected on Skype the more we realised that we were very similar and our work ethics were totally matching and we started to organise a real joint venture and started to travel interstate to work together. It has been such an amazing collaboration and as I mentioned before we are sisters and love spending time together and working together!

It's funny how things happen sometimes. One day Nat and I were chatting on her sofa, that's where the best ideas came to us, and we started to talk about me writing my first book. I used to call my training Meetup Mastery but I really wanted to change the name as the course itself was already a lot more than Meetups. I was actually teaching people how to create a following. Nat all of a sudden said, 'You should call your book FOLLOW ME!' OMG I loved it, perfect name.

So I decided to go along to Natasa's amazing Ultimate 48 Hour Author retreat in November 2015 to write my first book. I have dreamed about writing a book since I was a little girl and now it was really happening. Just 9 weeks later in early February 2016, I was holding my book and posted on Facebook a live video of me getting the delivery of my books and opening the boxes. It got over 1500 views in only a few weeks and I sold over 100 copies of my book instantly! I was so excited and humbled by people's excitement around my book.

But let me back track to the couch conversation with Nat. After she came up with the wonderful Follow Me name. I started to say, yes, yes it's perfect. People ask me all the time how I put bums on seats so quickly and that's what I wanted to name my course but one of my first mentors suggested that it was not a good catchy name, so I dropped it. Nat couldn't believe her ears as she was already planning to write a book about Bums on Seats too. She said, 'We should co-write a book sis! Bums on Seats!'

I loved the idea of co-writing a book with Nat, so I said, 'Let's make it a real project and record an online training with it and let's do a luxury retreat at the end of the year 2016 … BOOM!'

Nat and I got very excited about this idea and started to plan and decide when we were going to do this and how.

In December 2015 and January 2016 we both wrote our chapters and in February we finalised the book. We locked in some dates for recording and I found a great videographer to put the bums on seats online course together for us!

So on the 8th February 2016 Nat and I reunited and started to plan our amazing online course and on the 9th Feb we had a crew of 3 producers who come to Natasa's studio in Melbourne to record the 12 weeks online program Bums On Seats.

It was a huge project, as we had to record twelve 30-minute videos together and ensure we covered everything we wanted to say in 30 minutes. The producers were a little worried that we would not be able to record the 30 minutes without breaks or mistakes or cuts but as soon as they said, 'Bums on seats, cut 1, Mark' we were rolling and pretending to be LIVE and we just didn't stop for the 30-minute sessions. We did it; we rolled out the whole 12 chapters in a day. It was an intense day but as we love what we do we just kept going!

We did stop once as we were getting tired and we couldn't stop laughing when one of the crew started snoring behind the camera. It was hilarious and we just couldn't help ourselves!

Nat and I loved the recording day and they were very proud of us, we just match and work super well together, we could follow each other's conversations and flow from one subject to another. BOOM, SHUTTTUPP we did it!

As we were rolling we did have a few breaks and in one of them we did a LIVE Facebook post and we came up with an idea of a competition and we invited our followers to guess what time we were going to finish recording and the winner would win the first copy of the online program Bums on Seats! That was a super smart way to start selling the book to all the people who participated in the competition, as obviously they are interested in the program. That's why they joined the competition! Nat and I have a very creative way to sell our programs and to advertise them, we always do it by having fun and people buy more if they feel we are having fun and we are not hard selling to them!

Nat's take on Francesca

Everything Francesca shared is true to the word so I won't repeat the stories. All I want to share is the stuff that I have learnt and noticed on this journey Francesca and I are on. One thing that stuck out to me was the ability and courage Francesca had in outsourcing the stuff she was not an expert in doing so she can focus on the things that got her the best results. As a result, she helped me find a Virtual Assistant from the Philippines with her connections. This has been so freeing in my being able to also do the high quality business activities.

I have been in business coming up to 6 years now and never outsourced any admin work, which I sometimes had my dear husband do on my behalf. I did outsource but again not to the best person as Stuart is now better utilised in customer service and the more face-to-face stuff we deliver. I love that I took the leap and then worked out the 'how' with getting the Virtual Assistant. I know Francesca has two and an Executive Assistant that is with her now. This is something I admire, as the responsibility of having employees is huge.

I love Francesca's ability to think very quickly and resolve roadblocks and challenges that arise very frequently in running events. You must think quickly on your feet and find alternative paths. She is super quick and always in solution mode. This is a skill that has gotten us through many moments where we could have easily said – it can't be done or there is no other way. I work similarly to her, but her speed it something I admire in this aspect.

My final reason in wanting to write this book and create the other products around Bums on Seats is because I have never come across anyone in these past 6 years in business that put so much effort and focus in filling events and making sure people were having a great time every time. In collaborations things can be one sided often and this is an area I have had this experience on many occasions until I met Francesca. She has helped me so much in the past 8 months around building up my brand in Queensland and doubling the sizes of my events up there. Vice versa, I have been able to give back and help out with my network down here in Melbourne.

What are you going to get from this book?

You are going to learn how Nat and I creatively fill up our public events. We don't do just one thing. We actually do a lot more and in this book we show you what we do and how we do it. The Bums on Seats online program goes into even more detail and of course more interaction as you get to spend 12 half hours with us laughing, teaching and giving you clear steps on how to put bums on seats.

At the end of each chapter of this book you will get 3 take-aways for you to do and put in practice. So make sure you do the homework and not just read the book!

Enjoy the book and we hope to see you at the online course or at any of our courses or events. We both travel interstate a lot to the major capital cities in Australia so check us out and come along!

Part 1

Promote

Ultimate Brand Accelerator Masterclass - 2 Day Intensive

⚐ Public · Hosted by Natasa Denman

✉ Invite ▾   ✎ Edit   •••

🕐 March 22 - March 23
Mar 22 at 9 AM to Mar 23 at 5 PM

📍 Quest on Doncaster
855 Doncaster Road, Doncaster, Victoria 3108   Show Map

| About | Discussion |

Stuart, Andrea and 13 other friends are going

12	16	477
interested	going	invited

✎ Write Post   🖼 Add Photo / Video   📊 Create Poll   👤 ▾

Write something...

INVITE FRIENDS

+ Add friends to this event

Details

https://48.clickfunnels.com/ultimate-brand-accelerator-masterclass

After the huge success of our inaugural Ultimate Brand Accelerator Masterclass last October and amazing feedback from the attendees, we are excited to announce the new 2016 Masterclass.

Felicity Craig	Invite
Lendy Castillo Macario	Invite
Nikola Boskovski	Invite

1. Tribal Following

Francesca Moi

In this book we are going to show you multiple ways to fill up events easily, to be able to grow your business and your network. As you know, your network equals your net worth.

Let's get into it. Meetup is what I've used since October 2014 to grow my network to 12,000 hot leads and to create a 6-figure business. I started a Meetup group because I wanted to connect and find new clients without spending too much money on marketing especially since I didn't have any experience at that time. But what I found out was that I don't need to pay for any marketing, not yet, not until I had grown a powerful following.

So all I did was start a Meetup group (opposite page), start a community around my passion. I was a Life Coach at the time, and a Personal development group was a pretty good option to start from, and that group grew to 500 members in less then 3 months. I ran so many events and built so much trust with my community that in December 2014 I decided to start another Meetup Group called Entrepreneurs Abundance Mindset. After less than a year, I reached over 2500 members in total. Pretty exciting right?

You can also start a community around your passion around what your target market wants, and from there, they're going to know you, like you and trust you. You're going to be the organiser of the group, run events, teach them and add lots of value to the point that they're going to fall in love with you, and want to spend more time with you and spend more money with you. This is a no brainer, people buy emotions and if you spend enough time nurturing the relationship with them they are going to convert to clients.

The benefit of Meetup is that it's very cheap and it's free to be a member so your clients just have to come and get the chance to know you and trust to spend more time with you before they commit to a higher-end program. They don't have to have a big investment; they can just come along and meet you. For you to be an organiser it's only $14.99 per month, which is very cheap. For over a year and a half now in my business, lots of clients and friends were asking me, 'Francesca, what's your marketing budget? Looks like you're always online, looks like you're always so active.' And I said, 'Well, my marketing budget is $14.99 per month, which is my Meetup membership.' I know, pretty cool, right?

Another really big benefit of starting your own Meetup group is that Meetup.com is in 36 countries in the world, so you can really use Meetup to grow your network globally and to expand interstate like I did in September 2015 when I launched my Follow Me workshop in Sydney. Only thanks to Meetup.

Are you ready to do that? Because if you are, this is the place to be. Buckle up and let's do it.

Using Meetup to Grow Your Community

Meetup is a great, easy way to grow a community of raving fans. Before you know it, everyone will start to talk about you and will refer your business to their entire network. One of my clients from Melbourne started her first Meetup in October 2015. The feedback on the first night was, 'Oh my god, you're a person of influence, you look like you're so successful, Andrea, how did you do it?' Andrea literally called me and said, 'Francesca, I can't believe it, one event, and people already perceived me as successful. How did that happen so quick?' Literally, if you want your people to follow you, if you want to be seen as a person of influence, you have to do events, you have to start your own Meetup group and you have to invest time and grow your Network.

Meetup is a platform that is made for events. People who are already on Meetup will be notified through email to let them know about your event. It is advertising you, because of course they want their Meetup groups to succeed so that more people will buy their membership and start a group.

If you follow the steps in this chapter, boom, you can start your own network and you can be seen as a person of influence. When? Now! You don't need time, you actually don't need much; you just need to get started. So let's just do it!

Using Meetup the Right Way

Not everyone is using Meetup the right way. From my own research I found out that nearly 90% of the groups in Meetup in Australia are inactive. This is because people start a Meetup group thinking that boom, in a day they're going to be famous and then nobody goes along to their next Meetup event. The toughest

5

thing is how to get attention, and how to get people to see you who are actually coming along to the event after they RSVP.

There are a lot of Meetup groups out there and not very many are successful. There is a risk of failing in Meetup, but again if you follow what I'm teaching you in this book and if you follow my YouTube channels and look out for my tips on Facebook, and get the online Bums on Seats Program, I'm sure that you're going to be okay, that you're going to be able to succeed in your Meetups.

Stop working one-on-one with your clients and building your business on one too many strategies. Have you heard before of the marketing funnel? At the top you're going to have the cheapest things that people will get to know you from. Maybe your Meetup events, or emails, or YouTube videos, anything that you're going to create to get leads. Books, e-books, anything that people will get to know you through. Those go at the top of your funnel and then as you go down you start to charge a little bit more every time.

Your one-on-one time should be at the bottom where your highest investment program is. Instead, a lot of people put their one-on-one time straight after they first get to know you. They don't trust you enough to invest money in you yet. What you have to do is to make sure that you're going to build trust at the top and then once your potential clients and raving fans are ready, you offer them something like a half-day workshop or a little higher investment, such as a book in which people would not think twice to invest money in. Slowly build trust and offer bigger and bigger options to work with you.

Once they're ready, once they're warm leads, once they know you and like you, they're ready to come to the next level, which is still a one-to-many environment. You're not going to use your time with clients one-on-one, because then you're going to end up fully booked like I did in December 2014, and I didn't have any more time to take in any more clients, so my wage/income was capped by my own ability. I couldn't work 24 hours a day and my clients wanted me but I could only fit 10 clients a day for an hour each and that was already a bit of a long day.

7

What you're going to do is put the one-on-one at the bottom of your funnel and make sure that you build your workshops and your event that way, and offer your one-on-one time as an exclusive offer for elite clients. Of course all this would be once you have already got the confidence and the skills to do so!

Meetup in Detail

What exactly is Meetup? Meetup is the world's largest network of local groups. There are over 199,000 groups in 180 countries with 21 million members from 2001 with a monthly RSVP of 3.79 million. It's the platform to be in. Although Meetup is not the place you're going to go to teach people and get them into your book and try to sell to them, Meetup is a place where you create a community. Meetup is a place where members want to come and meet other like-minded people.

Remember that Meetup is not about your business; it's about a community. You have to be patient, you have to take time, you have to wait until the community trusts and likes you and then they will ask you how they can spend more time with you or how you can help them. I love it. It's like the dream of every Business Owner that like me didn't feel comfortable selling services yet.

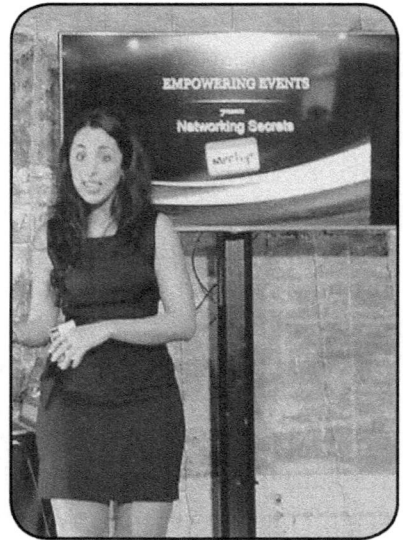

I attended one Meetup and there were probably 60-70 attendees there. It was fascinating, because nobody knew what they were doing there. Nobody knew why they were putting this Meetup on. There wasn't a goal for the community, the organiser didn't get the community together, they didn't give them time to talk to each other. It was all about the organiser teaching us something.

I mean it's great to learn something new, but at the end of the day if you want people to come back to your Meetup group you have to give them a chance to get to know each other, to create that bond between attendees. One person's going to say, 'I'm going to go back' and everyone's going to follow them. You have to create that strong bond between your members.

In fact, that group, at the end of the day we discovered that the organiser had a second thing in mind and wasn't upfront about it. I mean everyone has a motive to get more business, but if you're forward and upfront and don't just leave people wondering, that's when people are going to trust you and come back.

Frequency of Meetup Events

One of the biggest tips I could give you is that a lot of Meetup organisers, they do one Meetup a month and often they schedule on the Meetup group the whole year of Meetups. Now you can imagine if you do one Meetup a month, you're going to take a long time to build trust with your people.

Between one month to the next, things happen and people might forget about your Meetup and about you. They might forget to come along and they might go to another Meetup group which they find more exciting and where they meet more often.

If you do Meetup more often you're giving a chance to people to fill in their schedule. If you do it once a month and someone can't make it, there's no other chance for them to come until the next month. Here's what they're thinking: 'What if I can't make it? If it's been three months since I last came to your Meetup, I don't know, it's been a long time, I'm a bit shy, I'm not going back.'

You definitely don't want to do that. You want to do a Meetup every 10 days, as that will give them a chance to come along. Even if they miss one the next one is only in 20 days. They're not going to spend too much time without you and you're going to have more chances to grab more people. Especially for the first month or two. I actually did this for 12 whole months. Do your Meetup every 10 days. Nurture your members and give them value and they're going to definitely come back.

At the Meetup itself, you have to just give value. I'm not saying you have to do a presentation about your business. It's not about your business; it's about the community. What do they want to learn?

I'll give you an example of a bad Meetup. Let's say there's an accountant and all they want to do is show the attendees that they are the best accountant for them. If you do a Meetup like

9

this and do a presentation on how good you are, how great of an accountant they are, people are going to come along and say, 'Yeah, you're a good accountant, I'm not going to come back to your Meetup because I already know that this is what you're going to talk about every time.'

You're not giving a chance to create a community.

Step Back and Do Meetup Right

What you want to do is step back and look at all the things that your clients want. I understand that they need an accountant, but they don't know that yet. All they know and all they want is a marketing strategy, a business coach, someone who can help them get the money they need and want and once they have all those little steps done, then they're going to come along and say, 'Oh my god, Jim was such a great accountant, he gave me so many tips on how to do my tax, on how to put away my receipts, on how to have more cash flow in my business. He gave us so many tips, I now have so much money because of this Meetup that taught me so many things, the only person I trust is Jim.'

You have to build trust, give value and give tips. Do not do a presentation about your business, but just give tips away.

A lot of my clients say that they don't have time to do a Meetup every 10 days. What I can tell you is that I didn't have time either. I know it can be time consuming to run a Meetup every 10 days but I can tell you that, what if you don't go out there and create your own community? What if you don't create your own event? If you are reading this book most likely it's because you want to have more people attending your workshops, well let me tell you building a community is the best, easiest and cheapest way to do so.

You still have to go out there and network. If you go to a networking event and there are 40 people in the room, in 2 hours

10

they might give you half an hour or 45 minutes to network with other people. If you are lucky you're going to meet maximum 10% of that room, so that would be 4 people. If you run your own Meetup, if you run your own event one out of every 10 days, those people are going to hear about you. All the marketing that you're doing, everyone's going to hear about your Meetups and I can promise you that people will come eventually. They will come to see if you're doing a lot of successful events. Moreover, they want to know you, they want to be around you, they want to understand how you do these things.

I've got people who have followed me since 2014. They come along to my events, saying, 'Oh my gosh, Francesca, you were doing little Meetups for 4-5 people, look at you now. You get all those 60-80 people in the room with no effort whatsoever. It's so inspiriting to watch.'

You can do this too, it's very easy, and you just have to follow this one rule: consistency. If you're consistent with your Meetups, if you do a Meetup every 10 days, if you don't let your members down, they're going to commit to you and they are going to come back to your Meetups.

Objections to Creating a Community with Meetups

Some of my clients ask me, 'What's the point if I'm not selling? I need to sell. I want to do this because I need to sell.' What I can tell you is that all the Meetups where people start to sell straight away don't go very far. People get scared. They come to your Meetup, you sell to them, they say, 'Oh my god I'm not going to come back again, because eventually they're going to convince me that I have to buy blah, blah.'

What I can tell you is that once you've released the outcome of selling, once you just go back to your passion and feel that that's the right thing for you to do, to share your message, share your knowledge, then your people, the right clients, will come to you.

This can sound a bit airy-fairy, but it's actually not. Once you release the outcome of selling, once you are not as attached to money as an end goal, but all you want is to build a relationship and a community, I can guarantee you that if this is your intention, people will fill it and they will trust you. If your intention is just to make money out of this Meetup group, then it's not going to happen. People will feel that you have a second motive to do this Meetup and they're not going to come along.

Of course I'm not against making money. I grew a 6-figure business from this and I'm teaching you how to make a 6-figure business. The biggest tip I can give you is to not be desperate about money. Do not be attached to money. Let go of the outcome and trust that the money is going to come along once you're in touch with your passion and once you're balanced.

Fears That Come Up with Meetups

There are two fears that come up about Meetup. One is, what if nobody attends? This is a funny one. If nobody attends, nobody will know! I know, it's pretty funny, right? What you can do is just delete that Meetup from everywhere, nobody's going to know about it. Delete it from Facebook, Meetup, everywhere, just don't worry about it. Nobody needs to know that it never happened.

The second fear is, 'I don't have enough knowledge, I don't know what I'm going to cover every Meetup if I don't sell my business, I don't want to give all my tips away.' Well I can guarantee you that you have more tips and more knowledge than you think you have. To you, all the things that you know are obvious, but to your clients, they don't know what you know. They need to learn all the things that you know. A lot of the times, even as a business coach, a lot of people want to know how you spend your day, how you plan your day, how do you get things done, how do you organise yourself, how do you hire people, how do you choose how to hire people, and when do you know it's the right time for you to hire people?

There are infinite things that you think are obvious that you've done successfully in your business or in your life that your clients need to know. What I can suggest to you is that every single time a friend or a colleague or a client asks you a question that goes along the lines of, 'Hey, you're so good at this, how do you do it?' Write it down. Put it in your smart phone or a notebook where you just put all the questions that your clients ask you. Those questions are going to become a webinar, a presentation, a blog, an email campaign, anything, even your posts on Facebook. You can take these and really utilise them in millions of ways.

If you don't want to write it down, you can also record yourself and then get someone to transcribe it for you. This is very, very powerful.

Three actions I would suggest you do to be able to start your Meetup is:

1. You need to know how Meetup works before you start your own. Join Meetup and attend at least 3 events in the next 3 weeks until you're familiar with how Meetup works.

2. Look around at what your clients want. What are the types of Meetups they want to attend?

3. Once you're clear with that, you're going to divide a piece of paper, as seen below, into three parts:
   a. activities on the right hand side
   b. who's going to like this activity? in the middle
   c. left hand side is the name of the group that you'd start.

You're going to start to list the activities I mentioned before that your clients ask you. What are the things that you can talk about that your clients are interested in?

I also suggest you write a list of 20. From there you can go into the middle section and say, who's going to be interested in those activities? Once you understand who's going to like these activities, I want you to go deep. Don't just say 'business owners' that's not good enough. Go deep. Who are these business owners? Are they start-ups? One has a $200,000 business or $500,000+? Just define exactly who your target market is.

Then on the left hand side you can begin coming up with names for your Meetup groups, considering that the best formula to name a group is 'who' + 'what they want' + 'location'. An example: Entrepreneurs' Abundance Mindset Brisbane, Sydney, and Melbourne. That's my group that I grew to over 1,500 people in only 12 months. Go and check it out.

Do all the steps and make sure that you plan the next six months of your Meetups using those activities. Enjoy and don't procrastinate, just get going.

2. Sheep Effect

Francesca Moi

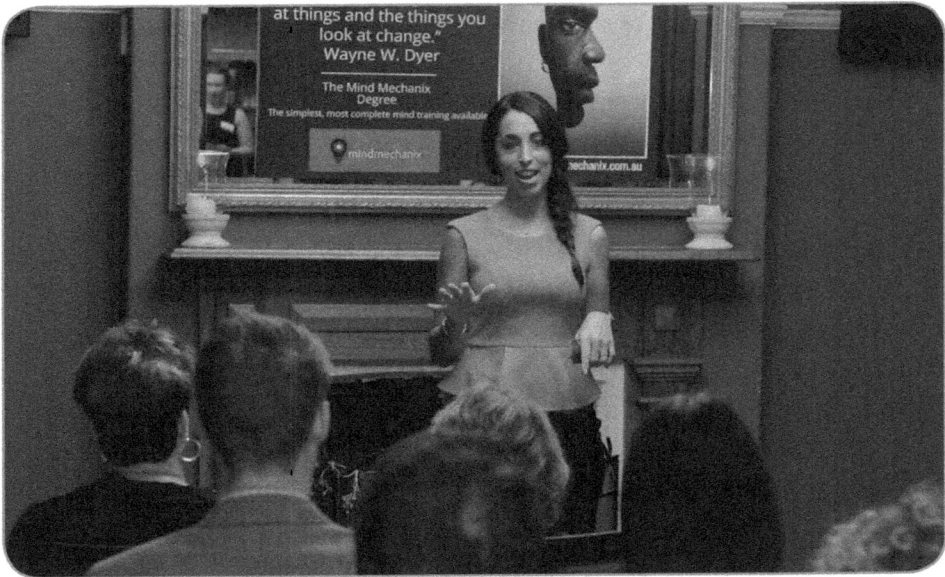

As you would know already a lot of people are followers, they prefer to sit and watch others succeed then take the rein and be the leader.

Of course, you're reading this book so most likely that means you are a leader by nature and you want to become an even better leader, so good on you for reading this book and taking the steps to expand your business and reach more people.

We're going to show you how you can create a following, because most people are followers. They love to follow leaders. I call it the 'sheep effect'. People love to follow the masses and their leaders. You have to understand that your clients will love to follow you and you have to be a great leader to be able to have the sheep effect working for you as well.

People Like to Follow Leaders and Other People Too

What's interesting about this is that they don't just like to follow you, they like to follow other people too. If there is an event where they can see there are zero people going or only three people going, they're going to think about how they're not sure whether it would be worth it to come along. But if they see that this event is really popular and everyone wants to go, they're going to think, 'Oh, there must be something good in this event, I'm going to check it out as I would hate to miss out.'

There is so much noise out there on Facebook, Meetup and all these different Social Media platforms that people are really struggling and don't know who to follow. Your goal is in fact to stand out so they will find you. Standing out for your crowd means understanding what they want and giving it to them in a very simple way. Be the face of their community. Be that person they want to come along and hang out with.

It's about creating credibility. If your target market or your favourite clients see that all the other clients are liking you, following you, interacting with you on Facebook and different social media, they are also going to start to do that. They're going to check you out and say, 'Who's this person who all my friends like? Who's this person who everyone is talking about?' You have to attract some leaders in your community, some people of influence in your community and everyone else will follow them. This is called the 'sheep effect'.

I always keep in mind and consider that before people commit to buying anything, they have to trust you. I imagine that they have different boxes they need to tick to get to make the decision to buy something. Everyone is different but most people would have these boxes to tick off:

- ☐ *Credibility*
- ☐ *Trust*
- ☐ *What other people think of you*
- ☐ *Perception*
- ☐ *Online presence*
- ☐ *Likeability*
- ☐ *Qualification*
- ☐ *Professionalism*
- ☐ *Resonance*
- ☐ *Public Figure.*

And a lot more.

Keeping in mind these boxes, every time I do something I ask myself, 'What is mßy intention here? What boxes would my client tick off if I do this or when I post this?' When I create this program, video, event, it's very powerful to understand the perception and the idea that other people will have about you. It's the same when you think about your event. Before they come along your clients will consider if:

- • *There are other people going.*
- • *Does it look fun?*
- • *Does it look Professional?*
- • *Does it look Interesting or boring?*
- • *Does it look like their money will be well spent?*

Would you really attend an event where there's only two people going? I know, right? No, me neither.

You have to think about why someone would come to an event on Facebook that looks like there are only two people going.

Why would someone join you in a Meetup when there's only one person going? Why would they be the first person to click? Would you? I wouldn't. I would be afraid to get stuck in, and stand out, and having the organiser expecting me to show up as no one else is going!

How you can change that for people is to have them create that momentum so that everyone else is going to follow.

Creating Momentum for Your Events

How are you going to do that? Well, let's find a way.

You could give away the first 10 tickets for free. Imagine you announce your next event and the first 10 tickets are free, people are going to grab the chance and you will sell out of the 10 tickets straight away! This will give other people the impression that this event is going to sell out quickly, so they are going to be more keen and committed to buy ticket 11!

It actually doesn't matter if 10 people get the ticket for free most likely those people are not even going to show up. But what you're giving is the appearance and the perception that there's already going to be 10 people going, so the other people, the other sheep, are happy to follow and commit and spend money on it, because there are already 10 people going. I will explain this concept in a few paragraphs.

This book is for you to stop working hard to fill events. Just work smart and not hard. Understand what your target market wants, understand what are the objections for them to commit to come along to your events and once you find that objections you can absolutely find a way to overcome them with no difficulties.

This book is also going to help you save a lot of money in marketing and get your raving fans ready. Create the sheep effect around you and create people following you, without you having to spend too much money, without you having to put in too much effort. Literally show them who you are; be real to yourself, be real to your people and they're going to follow you.

The thing that helped me the most is that I get a lot of clients coming to my half day workshop 'Follow Me' and they say, 'Oh my god, Francesca it's so good that you get so many followers.'

I have done this all on my own. There are a lot of very knowledgeable people, whom have lots and lots to give, they might have university degrees and might have very, very successful businesses, they know their stuff, they've got amazing knowledge but they haven't worked on creating a following. Now that business is shifting and becoming a personal connection with their clients they don't know how to stand out and how to be heard. Probably like you, you're reading this and I know you too have lots to give, people need to hear your story, but you don't know how to stand out, you might not know how to get people to your events or workshops.

It's very frustrating to see so much knowledge wasted, because people don't know how to get in front of other people. You have to get yourself an audience and they're going to listen to you. How do you do that? Create the sheep effect. Stay friends with your clients and keep giving value online and offline. Eventually when you have the trust you can also ask them a favour to put a little comment on your Facebook's posts or invite them to your next event and give them a free ticket. Give something, give to your clients, give to your people. I do totally believe that the more you give the more will come back. But you have to drop the expectation to give to get back. Just give with all your heart and it will come back! Make your clients feel special and they're going to help you by talking about you to their tribe.

Something very interesting is that we either, as business owners, don't really know how much we're worth sometimes. Or sometimes we actually value ourselves way too much. Which is great, but what I'm saying is that people don't know how valuable you are. People have been hurt before, people have been betrayed before, and people have paid money and then got a bad service. What I'm telling you is you have to build trust and you have to show your clients what you've got before you expect them to invest money in you. The best way is to create a following, to run your events, put bums on seats and that way you're going to be able to show them who you are.

How the Sheep Effect Works

Knowing about the sheep effect is a very smart way to boost the number of attendees at your events. It's right to call it the sheep effect because I've noticed that if an event on Facebook or Meetup shows only a few people attending, it was really hard for everyone else to join, but as soon as the number hit 10-15 everyone else was happy to invest money, to come along, to join the event, to click on 'going' and that would grow very rapidly. It's all about perception. People are afraid to come along to an event where there might be nobody attending.

If there's any uncertainty whether an event is going to be good, they're not going to waste any time. How do you do that? Absolutely you have to use the sheep effect. I've said that before, give away the first 10 tickets for free, it will change the number of your attendance very quickly. This will give you a chance to just go on Facebook or Meetup, send an email saying, 'Oh, wow, we just put up this event and within 10 minutes, the first 10 tickets are already gone, so make sure you get your tickets now, because they're going to be sold out by the end of the week.' Shut up. Boom!

Seriously, it's as easy as that. You're not lying, you give away the first 10 tickets, they're gone because they're free, everyone else is going to be ready to invest and come along to your event. If nobody joins you, if nobody actually takes the offer of the first

10 tickets for free, ask your friends, ask your clients to do you a favour. Ask them to RSVP, to come along and in exchange you can give them a half-hour free session. You can give them your book, or anything that you have that they value or that they want. In exchange they're going to help you a little bit with the sheep effect. The sheep effect works all the time. It's not only on Meetup, it's not only on Facebook, it's everywhere. People want to follow other people, people want to know that everyone else is coming along, so they say, 'Okay, I'll commit as well.'

The sheep effect is everywhere, not only running events. If everyone were waiting in line at public toilets everyone else will wait, nobody would go and check if all the cubicles are actually busy. They trust and wait patiently until one person checks because it's taking forever. People are afraid to stand out. The sheep effect is also on the road. Driving people follow each other like sheep; we all do it and have done it.

If You're Not Receiving, Give First

What if not even your friends and clients will help you with that? Well, okay sometimes the best way to do it and I've said that before, is to give first. If there's anyone else who is doing an event, just go on Facebook and share that event. Say to everyone, 'Hey, I've been to these events and I love them, why don't you come along with me?' The organiser of that event will be happy to help you and share your event as well.

Do not go out there and ask for too many favours, just give. Let go of the outcome, just give to other people and you will see that people will do it back to you. When I say, don't ask, I mean don't go to someone, some stranger and say, 'Hey, can you click here?' They might not do it first. Build that trust, that rapport, that relationship with them and they're going to be more likely to return the favour.

Why Give Away Free Tickets

Many people become a little bit greedy when I'm telling them to give away the first 10 tickets. The first 10 tickets are like bait. It's like when you go fishing and you put the right bait for the right fish. That's all it is. The bait is going to go. Of course it's a piece of fish and you might be able to eat it, but it's the one that's going to help you to get all the other fish, so you don't want to get greedy on those first 10 tickets, because those people are most likely not even going to show up. And if they do show up they're going to feel special because they've got free tickets.

Don't worry about that. Don't think scarcity, think abundance. It's not about the 10 free tickets. They're going to help you get all the other 60 people in the room. Trust me. Give it a go. The sheep effect always works.

And don't stop thinking about the sheep effect even when you are starting to get momentum at filling up events. Keep using the sheep effect, keep using the same bait. If it works don't change or stop to use a strategy!

Three actions you can take from this are:

1. Give away the first 10 tickets to your next event. Promote it on Facebook and Meetup. Tell everyone that the first 10 tickets to be booked for this event are free, but if you click on this right now and put your details in. Those people are going to get a free ticket.

2. Ask people of influence and friends to click on 'going' at your next event. Do it for them and they will do it for you. Get out there and start to create that following, start to create that interaction on your Social Media.

3. At your next event, on the night, tell all those people, all your attendees, they've already made an effort to come see you, tell them, 'Guys, the next event is in 10 days, we

are already promoting it, there's 10 free tickets. All of you can go online now and sign up to the next event.' How would that be perceived from the outside? You haven't even finished one event and the next event already has 10 others going? It's very powerful. It's a great way to get more people to your events, so make sure that for your next event you invite your loyal attendees to your next event. This strategy worked very well for me and it's a great way to make people think that if they come to the event they can get a chance to get free tickets. It's another incentive for them to commit and come along to your next event.

Go off and enjoy your next event.

3. Multiple Efforts

Francesca Moi

W hy would you do all this work of putting bums on seats alone, when you can collaborate with awesome people, other business owners, and other creative people and make a win-win situation for everyone?

It's just a no brainer. Get out there, find someone who you like, that you have the same connection with, you're excited to work together and you just know you want to work with them. Just go out there, find someone that's going to be great for your business and your growth.

There are so many benefits from collaborating with other business owners. You're going to join your brains, so you're going to work together towards success. It's not about competition; it's actually about collaboration. We should all be open to work together to help each other out to grow each other's businesses.

Two brains are better than one. You can work together and have great ideas, brainstorming. I'm going to tell you in a moment the story of Natasa and myself. We have been working together for the 9 months since July 2015 and it's been such a great, amazing opportunity for both of us and we've both learnt a lot from each other.

Natasa and I both love to learn new tricks and we are both doers. If we see that a strategy works for someone else we implement it straight away! The key of collaboration is to IMPLEMENT each other's suggestions and improve, grow.

It's always about creating a win-win situation and of course, it's about having fun. You can't collaborate with someone that you don't connect with energetically and that you don't have fun with. It's got to be fun and it's the best way to get in touch with and double your network. It's not just about one person, it's about both of your networks being put together. I suggest that you collaborate with people of influence, people who already have a big network.

Fears Around Joint Ventures

Many people are afraid of doing joint ventures, because they think the other person might steal their ideas or they think a person might take what they have to teach and they're going to take it and run with it. What I can tell you is that whatever you have, whatever your knowledge is, nobody can teach it as well as you do. Nobody's as passionate as you are about your own things. If it's your idea, if it's something that you created, that's your baby. Nobody can take it away from you. Even if they do take it they're not going to do as good a job.

There is no such a thing as COMPETITION, seriously competition does not exist, it exists only in our heads. Competition is just FEAR, fear of not being good enough, fear of losing clients to another person. We all have to believe and know that we are all unique, nobody can copy us, they can only use our ideas, but they can't do it the way we do it. They can only do better than us if we are not giving it 120%. If we have the certainty that we are doing the best we can and doing the things we know we should be doing then competition is not an issue.

If you are afraid that something like that will happen to you, it's time to not live in fear. I was reading the book of Oprah Winfrey, *What I Know for Sure* and on page 39 she says, 'Whenever I'm faced with a difficult decision, I ask myself, what would I do if I wasn't afraid of making a mistake, feeling rejection and looking foolish or being alone? I know for sure that when you remove the fear, the answer that you've been searching for comes into focus and as you walk into what you fear, you should know for sure that your deepest struggle, if you're willing and open, produces your greatest strength.'

This is something that I believe and I've been living it and it's become part of what I choose to believe every single day. What I suggest to you is that if you make decisions based on fear, you're actually not true to yourself, you're not going to attract the right things in your life. Don't be afraid of people who are going to steal your knowledge or your ideas, as that's what you're going to attract in your life.

If you work by yourself, if you just try to do it all by yourself, it's going to take you double the amount of time to achieve the greatest thing in your life and in your business. I've been in business for over 24 months and I can't tell you the number of people that I've been collaborating with. Every year I choose 2-3 people that I want to collaborate with, then over the year I just do one project or one event with them.

It's powerful and empowering, you can learn a lot from the other person and they can learn a lot from you. It's really the way to be working on your business at the moment. When I say collaborating, what I mean is anything like joint ventures, cross-promotional events, co-presenting an event or co-hosting it. Invite each other as a guest speaker at your own events, webinar and podcasts. Connect with anyone who's a person of influence and create that win-win situation, that bond that they're going to be able to share with their network and you share it with your network and everyone's going to get a win-win situation. They're going to get more value, they're going to learn something new and they're not just going to listen to you all the time.

Joining forces can be very powerful.

I've been doing a really amazing joint venture with Natasa Denman for nearly 9 months and now we're writing this book together and we have put an online program together also called Bums on Seats. We're going to run a retreat at the end of October 2016 as well. It's been a blessing that I've met Natasa late in July 2015.

Natasa and I met because I teach people what I actually do and I've been doing it the last two years and I knew Natasa had a big network. I knew that she seemed very genuine and very real from her Facebook posts and her Facebook videos. I really wanted to meet her and I saw that she was very successful as well. I knew that she was coming up to Brisbane, Gold Coast, from Melbourne and I friend requested her on Facebook. Natasa sent me a message asking me to go for a coffee and I said, 'Look, I'd actually love to run an event for you and have you presenting and teaching to my tribe.'

I didn't have an event planned in my schedule when I found out she was coming up here, but that's why it's great to have your schedule so that you know and you can play around with some dates and add dates if you need to, as in this case. I did that with Natasa and she came along and she had a really, really great event. We had 28 people there and it was really successful. From there we just clicked and realised that we could do great things together. We started to promote each other's events. I flew to Melbourne quite a bit and she flew up to Brisbane and I helped her fill up her events and she helped me fill up my events.

Natasa and I clicked and just knew that we are a match made in heaven and we were going to do bigger things together. We both work on the same high energy, having fun but also just getting things done!

It's about creating that win-win situation for everyone.

Creating a Community That Supports Each Other

Another way to collaborate is to create your own community that will support each other.

For example, I have the 'Follow Me' workshop where I teach people how to create a following. From there I teach people how to promote each other. The clients going on my two-day workshops are also invited to my secret Facebook group called Meetup Mafia.

We all help each other cross promote the same event. It's not just about doing it all by yourself, but I run an event and I tell the Meetup Mafia, 'Hey if any of your people will benefit from the event, can you please share this event on your Meetup or your Facebook?' Then everyone will help out and cross promote their events.

There's different ways you can do that for your own community, create that strong bond that people will start to work together and join in the collaboration.

Co-Hosting Events to Collaborate

Also I'm a very big fan of co-hosting an event. Let me introduce Mellanie Ballment. Mell is a dating coach, so we've got a slightly different target market, but at the same time it's great to create a following, to help grow your network so you can both fill events easier. All these collaborations are not only going to give you bums on seats but also they're going to help you to grow your networks so you can easily fill up events in your future.

Mell and I work together even if we don't have the same networks. Actually there are some single people in my network and there are some business people in her singles, so we can co-host an event. We help each other run the event and promote them. At a certain point we're going to be able to run a successful event.

Finding Partners to Collaborate With

If you're not sure where to find the next person you're going to collaborate with, I can tell you what I suggest you do or what I've done to find new people. First of all, networking is the key. You have to be out there, you have to do some networking events, you have to ensure that you're growing your network as much as you can so that people start to talk about you and people start to approach you and ask you to collaborate with them. I cannot tell you strongly enough how I feel about growing a network, because that's the way you're going to find the best collaborators and you're going to be able to check them out on Facebook and check out who you want to collaborate with. Who's going to be the one that your network is going to see as 'Wow, she's collaborating with that person. That's pretty cool.'

The way you're going to find the next person to collaborate with is to go to networking events, check them out on Facebook.

Look at people who run Meetup and other events – those are the people who you want to collaborate with. There's a very big fear that a lot of people have and it's commitment. If I start to collaborate with someone, what happens if we don't work well together? What happens if I realise that we're not really matching in values or not really thinking the same way?

What I suggest you do is write a contract, a legal contract, so if you decide to go separate ways you can separate your things and make sure that nobody loses anything. If you did make some money you can split it and all that. It's all done legally. That stuff for me is very boring, but I've got my lawyer, they do it, I don't have to worry about it and it's all done. Of course if you do start a collaboration, especially if it's going to make money or even just an exchange of value, you do want to put it in a contract so that if something happens you are both safe.

The best way to find other collaborators is to ask your network if they know anyone who's successful, or if they know anyone that's doing well in your network. Check out where people go, check out where your mentors go to events and networking spaces. Make sure that you are the first person who knows about what everyone does. If you don't know anyone, if you don't know what other people are doing in your network, it's really hard to find great collaborations.

People want to collaborate with people of influence. First of all, as I said before, grow your network, become a person of influence, become someone who people will want to be around and they're going to come to you and ask you to collaborate.

The three steps you're going to take away from this chapter:

1) Check out who in your network is a person that you'd like to collaborate with. Stalk them a little bit, not in a weird way, and connect with them. Do not just go there and say, 'Do you want to go for a coffee?' because they're going to say no. Those people,

if you're choosing the right people, are busy. They don't have time for coffee. But what you can do, as I said before, is give. If you know they have an event, just ask if you can help them on the event. Tell them you'd love to volunteer. Ask them, 'Do you need any help to put bums on seats? I can promote it for you.' Do anything, something that they need that they're going to find valuable to be connected to you. They might need some printing, to print flyers, they might need to have a lucky draw, they might need to find the venue, anything that they need, that you know that you can give, that's when you can contact them and say, 'Hey, I've got this for you and do you want it?' Do not go and ask for coffees, it's not going to happen.

2) The other thing I've done and again I don't want you to think I'm a stalker, because I'm not, but what I've done and it really works is to check out on Facebook where people of influence go. People who have got a big network, who are maybe successful businesses. More successful businesses than you. Go out to their networking events and collaborate and try to connect with them. Create a relationship. Do not do it in a sneaky way, do not try to get something out of them, just give and connect in a very open way. If you create a really strong friendship with them that's when you can start to collaborate.

3) Start to grow your network using Meetup as I suggested in the first chapter and start to create your strong collection of followers and they're going to help you grow your community in a way that the people of influence you want to collaborate with are going to come to you.

Use these three steps, make sure you go and start collaborating, think abundance and collaboration as the key.

33

4. Profitable Speaking

Natasa Denman

Being a speaker is one of the fastest ways to establish yourself as an expert and as the go-to person around the topic that you're speaking on. There are a couple of different ways you can speak in front of audiences. One is to be paid and another one is to do free speaking gigs. Normally when we begin in business we should be starting at a point where we're seeking out those free speaking gigs and working our way up to being paid for our speaking.

This allows us to build our muscle, being able to externalise our expertise and most of all it exposes us to many different people to build that 'like', 'know' and 'trust' aspect with us, so that they will do further things with us.

It's one of the fastest ways also to build your list with great, quality leads. It also builds your confidence, because no one is born a natural, extravagantly, amazing, eloquent speaker. People need to do, do, do. By being and by doing what great speakers do, then you become that person who performs fantastically on the stage. Repeat this over and over again.

Free speaking gigs are one of the most wonderful ways to get more bums on seats to your events, because people get to see a snippet or a taste of what you stand for and then they get to make that very next commitment to what you've got to offer. This perhaps might be a half-day event, or a two-day event. That very next step, however, should not be a very high jump from where you are, especially if you're on the stage for free.

By speaking for free, you grow your network. And as I said, you position yourself as that key person of influence around the topic that you're bringing. The beauty of it is that you're already in a room that is full of people who someone else has worked to get in the room for you.

They have promoted it, you just turn up and you do your thing. It's also a great way to build your brand and expose your brand to new people, frequently and at no cost. Did you know that sometimes you could make more from free speaking gigs in terms of revenue than paid ones?

Normally when you're getting paid for speaking, you get paid one fee and generally at the end of it there may not be an allowance to have that next step pitched to the audience as you are being paid for your expertise. However, in a free speaking gig, most of the time you would be allowed to pitch (I suggest that you check for permission first of all). If you can have that very next step advertised and then you get those people into a room with you for a longer period of time that is where the true relationship is formed.

As I mentioned, there are half-day events and full-day events, where you can further build their *trust, like and know* elements. Perhaps they will seek you out for further help by going into your higher end programs, which can be revenues way greater than just a single speaking gig fee.

Types of Free Speaking Gigs

What kind of free speaking gigs should you look out for? We suggest that you look out for networking events, certain expos that have speaking events on certain topics, being a guest presenter at other people's workshops to add value and a different angle to the common topic that's being spoken on.

You can also speak for free on podcasts. A lot of people nowadays are doing a lot of podcasts. They're putting it out there, building a big following of listeners and making great connections. This is another way to get a free speaking gig.

In the online world you can even have a fellow presenter or a guest presenter in your webinar. At interviews and sometimes at Meetup events they look out for speakers to come along and present.

The Key Elements of Free Speaking Gigs

In this particular chapter I want to share with you three key things for you to look out for if you are going to book out a calendar of free speaking events. Those events are then going to help you get those clients into the very next steps with you in terms of what you've got to offer.

1. What you must, must remember is that the focus is on relationships. If you have no relationship with those people who are the organisers of a particular event or the leader of a particular networking group, then you're not likely to be asked to speak at that particular event. The point is to get to know that particular person, more so than we suggest, in a friendly way. Know them like a friend and attend their particular event numerous times.

    This will help you get to know the structure, the people and the vibe of it all and to see if you really do want to speak there.

I want to share a story with you about when I met Francesca and how our relationship evolved from being online, just seeing each other on Facebook, within my group called Ultimate Business Support.

I saw Francesca post up a lot of different pictures of her doing Meetup events and running lots of workshops and events. I thought, 'You know what, this girl does a lot of events and so do I.'

She had friended me on Facebook and as I always do, when I accept a friend request I ask how we've met or connected and whether we know each other from somewhere. She just said that she had been following me on Facebook and she was part of my very big community there, Ultimate Business Support.

I was coming along to Brisbane, which is where she's based and I said to her, 'Look I'm coming up to do a couple of speaking engagements on these dates, I'm going to be up there for three days, would you like to catch up for a coffee?'

I didn't even put it out there that I was after her putting me in front of her audience, but because she heard that I was coming up and I didn't go straight for the intention that I always have in terms of connecting with influential people, I just said, 'Let's have coffee.' After all, you also want to check out if you are a good match with that particular person and you have that good energy.

Instead, she said, 'If you are free on that particular day, why don't I host an event for you and you speak to my audience and I'll pull something together? I'll host it, we've got a couple of weeks to promote it and you'll come up.'

As it turned out, I did go up, of course I accepted it and she had about 28 people in the room to watch me present for about 40 minutes. As a result of that, a person knew someone who was ideal to do my Ultimate 48-Hour Author Retreat, contacted him and he ended up becoming a client, pretty much within the following 48 hours.

This was a pretty astonishing turnaround from a free speaking gig, to get a client who wasn't even in the room. That's obviously a best-case scenario, but the point is, Francesca and I then continued to develop our relationship. We continued touching base. I then had her as a guest speaker at my 2-day Ultimate Brand Accelerator Master class and she did an amazing job, which resulted in her getting people into her half-day workshop and then doing her two-day high-end event.

The relationship continues to evolve and we continue supporting each other in our cities, because our networks are obviously a lot stronger, mine being in Melbourne and hers being in Brisbane.

2. The very next step to making sure that you monetise free speaking events is to ensure that you have got your funnel very clearly in your mind and as to what you would be offering at that particular free speaking gig. I always encourage people not to jump too high too fast, because the people who are listening to you speaking for free don't know you. Pretty much you're cold and you need to build that rapport and trust. Offering something that's $300 or less would be a nice next logical step.

    If we go back to the story I shared about Francesca and the very first event I did with her, my actual call to action wasn't to get an author into a retreat.

Obviously this was a best-case scenario and it happened and it's one of those 1/1000 situations. My actual call to action at that particular event was to attend my 2-day Ultimate Brand Accelerator Master class in Melbourne, which was being promoted, valued at $997, but at a special event price of $247.

People could attend and we run these three times a year now, which means that people can come along and join us and spend two days with us. It's a relationship building exercise, not so much about monetisation, because once the people have completed that 2-day Master class they tend to do those high end programs, retreats, masterminds, whatever it is that we have on offer at that particular time.

Those were the funnel steps that occurred at this particular event. What you need to look at with a free speaking gig is to invite them along for one session. If you're a consultant you give an outcome-focused name, as I say a sexy name that people will respond to. 'Okay, if I spend this time with you I'll get this particular outcome.' Either that or you offer a discounted ticket to one of your introductory events, which will then eventuate into those next steps.

3. The third thing you must ensure if you are going to make free speaking gigs one of your strategies to get bums on seats, which is super powerful, is to ensure that you follow up and stay in touch.

Following up is crucial. As soon as you've met people ensure that even in that room connect on Facebook, touch base on LinkedIn and so on. If you've promised anything at that free speaking event, which I always do, a great way to actually collect everyone's details in the room (make sure that you ask permission from the organiser) is to give something away, such as a free resource.

I normally give away my Ultimate 48-Hour Author book in e-book version and most people say, 'Yep, of course, I want a 160-page book to learn how to write my book in 48 hours.'

What happens is I say, 'Take out your mobile phones, pop in my mobile number ...', I say my number out and I say, 'Just SMS me your name and email address and I'll have it to you within 24 hours of this event and you can have a read of it.'

80-90% of the room all follow those instructions. Give them time to do it otherwise people will not want to put stuff in their phone while they're trying to listen to you. Either that or flash your number up on a PowerPoint slide and give them 3-4 minutes to complete that task.

This way you can have their names to connect with them on Facebook or LinkedIn or whatever other social media platform. They can then continue to follow your journey and vice versa; you're in touch with them. Send out that email or whichever free resource you have promised.

A big thing is to ensure that anything that you do in an event, especially a free speaking event, is that you run it past the organiser.

Tell them what your specific call to action will be. If you are going to do a data collection exercise like giving away something as a gift, always frame it as if it's a gift to the audience, rather than wanting to collect everyone's details.

When you've done this, ensure that it's nice to have a door prize. Sometimes if you can do 2-3 door prizes, everyone likes to win stuff and people will like you a lot better.

Be Well Prepared to Get Your Speaking Gigs

One of my biggest tips for you to gain more free speaking gigs is to go into your events well prepared with a speaker bio.

I've been around this industry for over 6 years and have noticed that people go in un-prepared to get their opportunities. A big suggestion that can help is to put together an A4 page 'speaker bio' (there's an example of one at the back of this book). Collate something like that so you can have it printed off and you can speak to the particular organiser about what you've got to offer and what some key topics are that you speak on. That way you're making their life easier; you've made the effort to build a relationship. You know what your next steps are and then you also follow up and stay in touch. You absolutely must do that. The key person who must always do that as well is the organiser.

Additionally, it's really great to connect with speakers who are speaking at other events, because obviously they've done the legwork to get where they are. You can ask them what they did to get the speaking gig, but also they may know of other places where they can recommend for speaking opportunities. If you make friends with influential people you will be able to recommend each other to other organisations and networks and all of a sudden you get booked out. You're soon going to need to be selective about where you choose to speak and where you choose not to speak.

Roadblocks to Getting Speaking Gigs

There's a lot of people out there who have been trying for a long time and they say, 'Look, I'm still not getting through and not getting booked as a speaker, even for free.'

What I suggest if that's the case and it's really about you, then to go back to the drawing board in terms of what your topics are. Change them all up. Also, if you've already got some established relationships, then go into those gigs with those new topics and test to see how that goes first.

If that doesn't change things, I would also change the groups that you've been approaching and try different groups.

You might have been getting free speaking gigs but there hasn't been any uptake of your next offers. You might kind of feel like all you're doing is free work and people are saying, 'Hey, that was great!' Yet, they're really not turning it into revenue for you. What I suggest that you do in this case is to change what your call to action is. Please keep it low risk, low cost in the early stages. People are just getting to know you and you may see a swing in your results.

It is about patience, about building your brand and how many people know of you. The monetisation will come in due course. If you're thinking that free speaking gigs are a waste of time, then I would like you to think again. It's actually probably your best type of activity that you can do, so that people are immediately positioning you in that expert status, because you're going to be introduced by the person who's running that particular event. As I said, with patience, you are going to get paid. There are no magic bullets, you've got to do the groundwork, you've got to hit the footpath running, you've got to turn up in front of people and you've got to get known. After all, that's what the politicians do. When they run such huge and long campaigns others know them and then others start contacting them, swinging their way as we say.

I trust that has been useful, this strategy is probably in my top three that I use to fill my events and get bums on seats. Go out there and set a goal of what it is that you're going to achieve and how many speaking opportunities you are going to find in the next 3, 6 or 12 months. Set the goal and once you have that focus, gigs and opportunities will start to open up and come your way.

5. Engaging Emails

Natasa Denman

Keeping in touch with your audience is a crucial part of building those relationships long-term. Email marketing has been around for a very long time now and even though it's losing its effectiveness more and more it is still an important part of your strategy to get bums on seats.

When you meet people online or offline and they request to receive information from you, we call this someone 'opting in'. They are therefore interested in the information you have to share. This is also the beginning of your sales funnel. Your email marketing lets your database know about your upcoming events, numerous times, as it is a key to get your followers to come along and actually spend time with you in a live event. It's a great way to add value to your audience as well, which is what I would recommend you do on a regular basis, in addition to promoting your events.

Realistically, your email marketing needs to be created around storytelling, which is engaging for people to have a read through. Really the promotion should only be about 10-20% of the email content, perhaps even just put into the P.S. statement at the bottom of your email. Sometimes you may have something to announce that's quite 'a big deal' and you might want to build up the hype around what you're announcing. On most occasions though, storytelling should be the key focus of how you send out emails to your community.

Staying Top of Mind with Your Audience Through Email Marketing

It's a great way to stay top of mind with your audience. In the last 6 years I've been in business, sometimes I've had people become clients after being on my email list for as long as 4 years. A lot of the time they've been on the list for 6-12 months through to 2 years and because they keep getting my emails and I kept appearing in their inbox, my business and my name stays somewhere in their subconscious mind so when they do require what I've got to offer, they know exactly where to go and who they perceive to be the expert in that particular filed.

It's a strategy that you must practise patience with, especially in the early days while you're building that database and increasing your numbers. It's really one of the 10 most powerful ways to get bums on seats and that warm audience to come and spend that time with you and they are more likely to take that next step into your high-end programs.

I always encourage people to share information and insights with their database so that the database doesn't feel like they're being constantly pitched at.

Announce it Once and Forget About It? No!

When it comes to an event, in my early days in business I used to only announce it once and I'd wonder, why didn't anyone book? Or maybe just 1-2 people expressed interest and it made it really hard for them. This is not what you do. You're not to send out an email and say, 'Oh look, if you want to come to this event then email me back and I'll send you an invoice and the details.' It really needs to be one click away. Your event must be set up, either on your website, or on sites such as Sticky Tickets, or Eventbrite, which are free to use. These sites keep a commission of the tickets sold, so that you're able to send through an email link where people can go directly and the next step is to purchase their ticket for the event.

This is the number one essential key thing if you want to get more people to click through your emails.

Even before that you need to get them to actually open the email! So number two is for them to click on that link and be able to register as quickly as possible.

Getting Good Responses to Your Events through Email Marketing

The fact is you need to be sending out a minimum of 3-5 emails as a sequence to get a good response to an event. Obviously if you're running a lot of events, after a while you will exhaust your list, perhaps most of the people who were going to come have already come. That is why when we talk about paid advertising, that's why you tap into more of a cold market and continue building your database to have more people coming through and becoming warmer leads as they're being communicated with.

If you don't make email marketing one of your key tasks that you perform to build your business, then you'll be missing out on this free strategy to get bums on seats. People will not remember or think of you. What I'd like to always say is that you want to possess some kind of real estate in some people's minds for the expertise that you possess or the solution that you solve.

With Ultimate 48-Hour Author that's exactly what we do with people and when they ring us, these are the things they say to us: 'I've seen you around for so long, I get your emails, this person

49

talked about you, everywhere I go people are mentioning your brand.' I possess real estate and space in that person's mind, so if they wanted to write a book, we're the right people to approach, because we've appeared left, right and centre.

If you don't make this part of your strategy as well, your numbers will definitely be lower in your events and you'll definitely have less raving fans. Email marketing really nurtures those people who are following you and reading about you and following the whole journey that you're on.

Strategies for Email Marketing

What I want you to really be able to take away from this chapter is how and when to send out those sequences of emails to really promote your events, so that your audience also feels that they've received value as well as being advised about what's coming up from your end.

1. How many steps should you have for an event and what is the timing of when you should send them out?

    Normally if you're running a webinar, give yourself 7-10 days lead up time and send out 3 emails. The first email may go out, 7 days to go, the next one 3 days to go and the next one 24 hours to go. With an event we're generally saying, give yourself 4-6 weeks lead up, with a sequence of 5 emails that might come 6 weeks out, 4 weeks out then 2 weeks out, 1 week and then 3 days out. If it's a live event, generally sending communication 24 hours out, people will have already set plans in place for whatever they're doing in their everyday life. That's why 3 days out would be the closest promotional email that I'd send out for a live event.

    If you're running high-end retreats, then certainly I'd advise people to actually report back from the high-end retreats as they're running. Have a bit of storytelling happening and then people can inquire about the next one. It's not really necessary to do lead up emails to the high-end retreats, because realistically you should be filling those through your low-end events where you've built that trust and rapport with people in the room.

It is most likely that people will sign up into your high-end programs through having met you. It's very rare that people would phone in or come through an email, or just because they've found your website to invest tens of thousands of dollars with you.

2. Ensure that you're writing valuable content. One of the questions I get asked is, 'What do you write?'

   You can report back on different case studies, using or sharing a testimonial, sharing an interesting fact, anything that may have happened in your everyday life so you can twist it in a way that fits with whatever you're about to have a call to action for. Copywriting is a skill that a lot of people are scared of and what I always say is the more you do it, the better you get at it. If you actually read someone else's copy that you really enjoy, there is a trick to getting good at it. That is if you rewrite the exact same thing the way that someone else has written it, a few different times, your style of writing can change to sound more the way they have written it, so modelling that aspect.

   I read that in a Tony Robbins book where he said to write out something, just copy it word for word, obviously not putting it out there, this is just for practise and then put it out there when you have written it in your words and style. I remember when I handed over my copywriting to my husband who then took over all my email communication and he said to me, 'Wow, you're

51

so good at writing this stuff, the sales copy and telling the stories.' And I said, 'I've been doing it for 2-3 years.' Nowadays that I haven't done it as long for our business, the last three years he's been doing it and he's just gone up leaps and bounds and writes amazing copy.

As the saying goes, the being comes with the doing. The more you do it, the more you find people you know who enjoy how they write their copy and then model that. That's how you will be able to become a great content writer and deliver amazing value to your email list or your database.

Last of all ensure that you're using some kind of a platform where you can set up sequences on autopilot. They call them customer relationship management systems (CRM) and there are so many different ones out there. The most popular ones, to mention 2-3, are MailChimp which has a free version and has amazing templates, if you want to do newsletters or have a really good look to your emails, you can use that, however their autopilot component would be a paid version of that particular platform. We have used Send Pepper as our CRM since we began, there's Constant Contact, and AWeber, those are just a few and then the more high end ones, InfusionSoft and Office Autopilot, which cost around a few hundred dollars per month and they've got a few thousands dollars set up fees, but they're very sophisticated CRMs.

If you're early on in the business, start off with something that's perhaps around the $30 US per month mark and work your way up as your business grows. It's great to invest in something like that because it does give you amazing reporting in terms of who's clicked and how many people have opened your email. Some of them can take payments and have all sorts of steps set up, which are quite sophisticated.

You can choose to outsource to someone if you don't want to learn it yourself, however I think a simple version of a CRM, like MailChimp or Send Pepper can be learnt and mastered quite easily just by following a few videos and in the early days you can utilise it yourself and save some money that way.

Down the line when you have a lot happening and you're outsourcing to a virtual assistant, it is recommended that you could be spending time on the money-making activities.

A really hot tip for email marketing is to ensure that you have a sexy, catchy, subject line. Most people will open emails according to the subject line and if it's not catered or makes them curious enough to want to open it, then they're likely to just click 'delete'.

In my time a few of the popular subject lines that are quite generic that you might want to trial are the ones that people open the most, would you believe, is 'Bad news'.

Another one that's really highly opened is 'Final notice'. Subject lines like that are more likely to spark your reader into opening your email. Don't simply call it a 'monthly newsletter'. Make them really curious to want to go inside and actually read the content and ensure that you engage through your content.

If you're going to put down the subject line, 'Bad news', explain in the first couple of sentences what you meant by that, even if you're turning it around. So the 'bad news' is this, the 'good news' is this etc. etc. and go into it that way, as people will feel cheated and they will certainly unsubscribe if you haven't explained yourself, especially if you're doing quite controversial subject lines.

If you are doing email marketing and you find that no one is booking, I would go through and ask yourself a few questions. Check first of all the open rates of emails and if people are clicking through on the link and then also whether you've set up enough emails to go out for the event.

Have you only sent one? Have you sent multiple emails? Then last of all look at the content and try something different. If you haven't been telling stories and all you've been doing is promoting, how about then just telling your story or a zero to hero journey of one of your clients that has achieved the success that you helped them achieve.

Unsubscribes. People worry about unsubscribes, because people may feel like they are being spammed. I say embrace when people unsubscribe or even complain, because it means that you're doing enough marketing, it means that your list will be cleaner and you'll be more relevant to those who want to hear from you and if you're telling stories then people won't feel like it's spam, it's just that they don't require what you've got to offer and perhaps it's just filling up their inbox from a lot of emails that we receive nowadays.

What to Outsource?

Last of all, some things I recommend you outsource straight away. The simplest CRMs are really easy to learn through videos, however, as you get busier and understand how to use them I do recommend that you outsource it to a virtual assistant. That way it's all set up and run for you and even just to record a message and send it to your VA and then they can compile something for you and create it for you.

There are virtual assistants out there who are great at writing emails and copywriting. That will be something that you can outsource fairly quickly or early on in your journey. Just see how things go and the results they are getting.

Most of all, keep your finger on the pulse, see what results you're getting, if you're getting poor results and not changing your strategy make sure you try something else. Ensure that you're always planning a number of emails to promote a seminar or webinar. With retreats when you're sharing what's happening, you want to be getting people curious enough to contact you and speak to you about it.

MONDAY NETWORK | TUESDAY VALUE OFFER
WEDNESDAY VIDEO | THURSDAY RECOMMEND
FRIDAY CELEBRATE | SATURDAY PERSONAL
SUNDAY INSIGHT

Ultimate Business Support
Instant BAN if you Spam!
2016
Ultimate Success!

Ultimate Business Support INSIGHT
🔒 Closed Group

Joined ▼ | ↗ Share | ✓ Notifications | ...

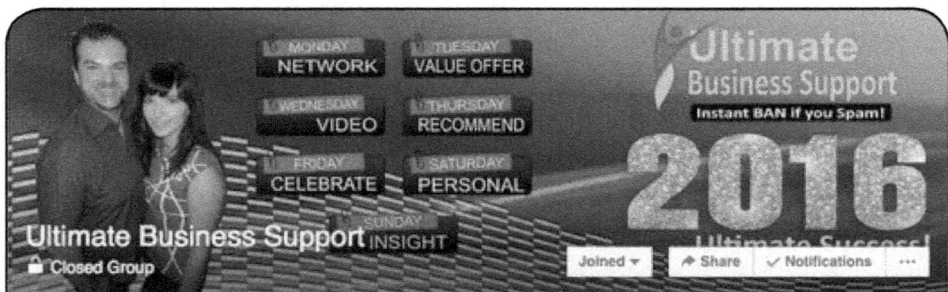

Discussion · Members · Events · Photos · Files

Search this group 🔍

📝 Write Post | 🖼 Add Photo / Video | 📊 Create Poll | ⊕ Add File

Write something...

PINNED POST

Natasa Denman
January 25 · Melbourne

Coffee Chats with Nat & Stu for all UBS Members MONDAYS 9AM... Each Monday you will find myself or Stu online for 30 Mins at no cost but tons of value and insights shared from behind the scenes of how we really make things happen in our business and how you too can model it for yourself.

Register Once for the Full Year of calls and come when you want - reminders get sent out regularly. Here is the new code for 2016: https://attendee.gotowebinar.com/regist.../7003636553402720257

Sometimes Live Streamed via Periscope @natasadenman

COFFEE CHATS MONDAY'S

ADD MEMBERS

✛ Enter name or email address...

MEMBERS   11,512 Members (49 new)

Invite by Email

DESCRIPTION   Edit
Hey there! If you are here it's because you want to propel your... See More

GROUP TYPE
Support

TAGS   Edit
Small business · Marketing · Coaching

CREATE NEW GROUPS

Groups make it easier than ever to share with friends, family and teammates.   Create Group

UPCOMING GROUP EVENTS   See All

MAR 15 | Adelaide Ultimate Business Support Live Event
Tuesday, March 15 at 6:30 P...

6. Facebook Impact

Natasa Denman

Building a community and tribe is a powerful way to engage your audience and to continue building those relationships in an online forum, whereby you don't need to be out and about connecting with people via coffee chats. That's why creating a Facebook group has been the most transformational thing for my business, which occurred about 3.5 years ago when I was working with my second mentor. She suggested that I start this open community where I invite my current clients and people in my network and then I build it up so that it starts attracting new clients and customers. But more so, initially connections would come that I could build a relationship with over a period of time.

Through having a Facebook group you're able to add value to people by maintaining those relationships with more consistency. You will definitely be able to promote your events regularly. Your community will be able to connect with you offline and that is how you're going to obtain more bums on seats for your events. Facebook groups are a really amazing testing ground for creating new events and webinars and different offers for your business. If they are successful and have a great uptake, then you can take that out in the offline world and promote it in the same way with the same outcomes.

Facebook Groups are Great Business Support for Everyone

Being part of a Facebook group, especially if it's your own, will give you support from other experts in areas you're not an expert in. When you're stuck you can get answers to your questions fairly rapidly and discover a lot of joint venture relationships on the way that can open up for you in your business.

Many people ask, what kind of groups should I create and become a part of? If you don't know, then go and hang out in groups where your ideal clients' interests are and solve their pain. When you're creating a group, do keep it simple and a little bit more highly chunked, so more broad.

Our particular Facebook group that we started 3.5 years ago is called Ultimate Business Support. The biggest challenge for small business owners and solopreneurs is that we are alone and looking for that support from people around who can help answer some of the questions that we have.

We kept it quite broad and their interest was in finding support in having a community. Through various posts and insights that I shared throughout the months and days that we've been running this they have built quite a strong connection with me. When I am putting out those offers or promoting my events there's a certain amount of uptake for them to come on and spend some offline time with us.

Promoting Your Offline Groups Through Facebook

After the Facebook group got going we started running an offline event, initially just in our home city of Melbourne and it's now evolved and run in Sydney, Adelaide and in Brisbane. Those people who attend live are now connecting and hanging out together offline, which is absolutely fantastic and a great way for them to grow their business.

Strategies to Manage

I want to share with you a few different strategies on how you need to think about your own Facebook group and I highly recommend that you do start your own. Then you need to nurture it, be there and be the leader, because it's just another fantastic positioning tool of you being the expert and that key person of influence.

1. During the structure and the building stages of your Facebook group, initially you have to think about who this is going to be for, what they are interested in, what their pain points are and how you're going to solve that problem. Ultimately you're that expert that they're going to go to when they need the solution to their problem. During the building stages, you will want to learn how you get people to post on your group of their own accord.

   Many people feel uncomfortable in that they don't know what to post. They don't ever post; they just sit there in the background watching. How are you going to engage people? Is it going to be through questions, is it going to be through competitions, pictures, videos or sharing some personal elements? What we did in our group is to create theme days so that people knew what they were going to be posting every day and what was suitable to post. I found many people wonder if what they're going to post is okay to post in a particular group, but if they were going to have some particular theme that they could adhere to it would be really easy and interactive for them to go and get involved.

59

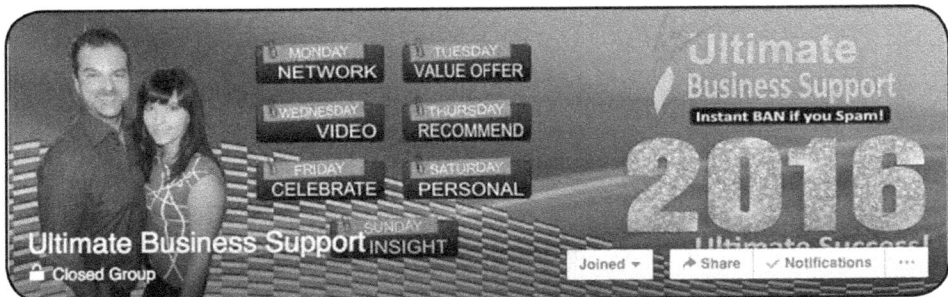

We also ran competitions where I was giving away one of my books for every 100th person who joined the group or referred others to the group. The current members went into a draw to win a book and I did a short video to announce who that particular winner was, which was very interactive.

2. Engagement is the second step, which is hugely important and very crucial one for the group's longevity. What you can find in a group of hundreds or even thousands of people is to have no one posting on it and that can make people leave and go elsewhere. It could have been just the organiser or admin person posting time and time and time again, which is not the point of a community, as no one feels important. A community should be able to sustain itself, it will have its peaks and troughs, however it should be able to allow you to go on holidays and come back and it's still running hot and people engaging with each other and that everyone is getting some kind of outcome from it.

Often with our Ultimate Business Support group we get a lot of inbox messages from members to say, 'Hey I sold my package for this particular thing through the group', or 'I've been able to gain so much business from your group, so thank you so much for putting this group up.'

Just ensure that you are the leader of the group, so by being the leader you need to commit to posting 5 out of 7 days, if not every single day, according to your theme. Unfortunately, on Facebook groups you cannot schedule posts, so you do need to go in there and post them manually. The beautiful thing about them is they are a two-way conversation. Different people can post and they can reply to comments. It's actually people interacting over the Facebook fan pages, which is more like a business page that talks to people, but doesn't have as much interaction as in a group.

3. What you must be careful with and another key thing around Facebook groups is the management of it and how you handle spam. You will have people coming and posting things that you may not want there. Perhaps pornographic images, network marketing, online scams and even promotional posts when they shouldn't be posting promotional posts.

   How will you manage new members? Will you welcome every single new person that comes into the group? Will you ask them a question? How will you do all of those things so that you appear consistent and so that you're positioning yourself as the leader?

Facebook Group Promotion Through Consistency

My favourite saying is 'consistency is king' and you must show people how much you care, before you show them how much you know. Just looking after people and ensuring that it's a nice clean group, with people who are posting valuable information for the others in the group is one of the keys to ensuring that the community continues growing and striving.

If Facebook notices that your group is interactive, they will promote it out themselves to a wider audience. In this case you might have a huge influx of people coming in as members. I do suggest after a little while if you are creating a group as an open group that you change it to a closed group. This way only members can see the posts within the group. If you are creating groups that are going to be just for paying clients that you create them as a secret group.

Our recommendation is that you have one for the wider community and people who don't know you can come in and join and that you then have certain Facebook groups for all your paying clients. For us, particularly, we call that one the UBS Inner Circle and that's where all our paying clients hang out away from the group that's got almost 13,000 members.

Boosting Your Facebook Group Numbers

Our hot tip around creating a Facebook group is to add as many of your friends who would benefit from the group first. Then you can put up a mix of 15 different posts before anyone arrives at the group, because that way new arrivals can see that where they have been added is already an active group. If they see valuable posts then that's absolutely amazing.

Then you can also get five of your close friends to post, so that it doesn't look like it's just you posting post after post after post. In terms of your events there is an option in every single group to actually post your event within that particular group. That way you ensure that you're getting a lot more bums on seats to your events. This is a very powerful way through which my group has become almost like a second lounge room, where we go and hang out with that particular community. We're not able to all see each other, as we're spread all over Australia and the world, it's become all about nurturing and having that consistency, being there, for a long time and being a stayer.

Reasons Why People Don't Interact in Facebook Groups

It's tough if you have started a group and you're finding that there's no one interacting. You might be feeling that it's just a little bit silly, that it's like talking to a wall. You might be feeling that all you can hear is the crickets chirping. In this case challenge yourself to do something different.

If you've been doing the same thing over and over and you're not getting interaction, then you need to do something different. Be really brave and post something that you would never post. Go on other groups that are interactive and have a look at what the admins are doing in those groups to get their crowd or their tribe engaged and then keep testing, especially also in your early days, if your group is quiet, it's about patience, people are just observing if it's a safe place to actually voice their opinion or post a particular post.

Some people say, 'Hey, managing a Facebook group takes too much time, I can't be bothered, you have to be on there all the time.' I always say, 'Look, building the foundations is where the time is, once it's well established and has good interaction, you can go on holidays over Christmas when people tend not to be as much on social media as they're hanging out with their family and friends, it will still sustain itself with those who are still around.' As I say, every beginning is hard. In the beginning it's awkward, it does take a lot longer to master, but it's certainly worth it. It's going to be one of your most powerful ways to get that community to attend your events.

Managing Spam on Facebook Groups

Last of all, people have a lot of trouble managing the spam and people can be really tricky in the way they post a certain post that revolves around ultimately having a pitch and being promotional. You just have to be very careful and if people are using every single day as a way to promote in a clever, written format or through a video, then I suggest you just watch out for them, warn them and if they don't take the warning you can then ban and delete people out of groups. Do keep your group clean, because you want people to stay and be part of it for a long time. We have seen over 3.5 years people come and go and leave and come back again. This is great to see, because they're seeing some kind of value so look for different ways that you can engage them.

Another tip for you is last year we started doing 'coffee chats' on Monday mornings via the GoToWebinar platform. We would just sit and chat to our members who wanted to turn up and ask business support related questions. That's how I was connecting with them in a more live and personal manner. It added a lot of value and converted into business. I would announce what were the next gigs that were coming up and then those who were interested would take that particular offer or come along to our upcoming events. It was a really great way to fill our offline events, a great way to fill our other promotional events that my business was running.

Natasa Denman
January 25 · Melbourne, VIC, Australia

Coffee Chats with Nat & Stu for all UBS Members MONDAYS 9AM... Each Monday you will find myself or Stu online for 30 Mins at no cost but tons of value and insights shared from behind the scenes of how we really make things happen in our business and how you too can model it for yourself.

Register Once for the Full Year of calls and come when you want - reminders get sent out regularly. Here is the new code for 2016: https://attendee.gotowebinar.com/regist.../7003636553402720257

Sometimes Live Streamed via Periscope @natasadenman

Blaise Van Hecke, Irene Scott and 16 others   3 Comments

👍 Like   💬 Comment

64

There are so many things that we're sharing with you in *Bums on Seats,* where you can choose to engage as your strategy to get more bums on seats. We're just sharing with you the ones that work really well. If they're not working for you, the question to ask is, have I been consistent, have I really given this a red hot go for a good period of time and if it's not working, what else can I adjust so that it does start working? It does work, we know it and it isn't just myself that has been able to make it work. Francesca has her own very interactive group and she uses all of these 12 strategies in these 12 chapters that we've shared to run super amazing events.

7. Raving Fans

Natasa Denman

Having fans is not exclusively available to the celebrities, movie stars, singers and people who are in the media. You can become famous in your own right. If you do the right thing, if you position yourself right and do things because they're hard, not because they're easy, people will start noticing that. They'll start following you, liking you and talking to others about you, even if you don't know that is happening.

In their early days on Social Media people say they post so much and they don't get any responses from their friends or even acquaintances. I always say you have to play the patience card. You have to really prove yourself to the public and the people who are observing your journey, before they start to interact and say how they have been following your journey or how inspired they have been by you.

It is really flattering when you have people coming up and asking for your autograph, because you've written a book as we have. Many also want to have a photo taken with you or they send you a private email or message that says how much impact you've made on their lives.

Increasing Your Credibility With Raving Fans

Having raving fans really enables you to build your business. More importantly it becomes so much easier to get those bums on seats in your seminars. Your raving fans will return numerous times even to the same seminar, which gives you a lot of credibility in the eyes of the people who are new to your world and are just beginning to start the relationship.

They've really increased your credibility. Your level of trust and rapport that you can build with others grows a lot speedier. They work for free to give that reference for your events and seminars and they become like a salesperson on the road for you. It's really important that you invest some time to nurture those relationships, because ultimately they'll help you out even more.

It could be as crewmember at your events, which again makes you appear a bigger star and more professional. They will support you in your Social Media posts by creating interaction and engagement, which means that your posts will get pushed up a lot higher. They're more likely than anyone else to invest in every single thing that you bring out in terms of a product or service.

At the end of the day, raving fans are to be looked after in the best way you can. From time to time give them something as a 'thank you' and support them in your community, because their value may be intangible, but huge in regards to the exposure they create for your business.

Invest Time in Building and Nurturing Relationships With Your Fans

If you do invest time in building and nurturing those relationships, it means you'll have to spend less money on advertising and you'll get a whole lot more word of mouth referrals, which is actually the strongest and highest percentage that are likely to convert to sales.

Raving fans are people who really embrace what you do and how you do it. They speak to others about you in high regard and will drop most things in their life to spend time with you. There are different extremes of fans and we'll cover that later on, but I want to give you strategies on how to nurture those relationships and support them so that you both may grow and benefit from the relationship.

The very first thing I would suggest you do is connect with your raving fans online and offline, treat them almost like a referral partner and build that closer relationship. Make a phone call from time to time, they'd like to hear from you, as well as then invite them to your offline events. Often times they'll be the first ones to put their hand up to crew for you and be part of the behind the scenes stuff that happens.

Ultimately, they'll learn a lot about how you do things and eventually you may be able to tap into having someone as a casual or part-time employee as your business grows bigger and bigger. Do create a lot of engagement and a two-way conversation between those people who seem really engaged, but more importantly don't be afraid to ask for help. That is one

69

of the key ways to actually get people to like you. Psychologically, if we ask someone else to do us a favour and they obviously comply with it, they in turn end up liking us a lot more.

Just think about the last time someone asked you to do them a favour, how do you feel about that person right now? I use this strategy in my events and my speaking gigs. Very early on in doing an event or a speaking gig, I actually ask the audience to do me a very small favour.

For example, you could ask the audience to get up and sit next to someone totally different. At the beginning you can say: 'Can everyone do me a small favour please?' If you also give them a good reason why it will work even better. It has to be within the context of what you're doing, but if you do that with the audience they seem to have more of an inclination towards liking you and building that rapport and trust a lot faster.

That's a little hot tip to get them to engage with you more rapidly. Do it at your events, do it at your speaking gigs and absolutely, as you ask people for help, in turn they will like you a lot more. Continue this strategy ongoing.

Recruiting Help at Your Events

Francesca has said that often people come along early at events to be in the room, to obviously network from the beginning. If you're the person who's arriving early at an event, ask the organiser if you can give them a hand. If they say no, ask again. I like the fact that Francesca said that, because often people feel like it's an inconvenience if you want to help them. If you ask a second time they're more likely to say yes, because you affirm that you're really putting your hand out and saying, 'I'm willing to help you.'

I really love that tip, so whenever you go to an event, our recommendation is to always arrive a little bit earlier. Not too early, just 10-15 minutes earlier and offer help, because that's how you will build up a lot more rapport with the organiser. Perhaps you'll even get to meet the speaker, because speakers usually arrive earlier as well to set up for the event. That's where you can become kind of on the inside, behind the scenes, without being an official crewmember.

Be Yourself and Lead by Example

Last of all, how do you build a raving fan base? The answer is: be yourself. That's what I always say. If you can truly and honestly say you're just being the most unique version of you, that you're leading by example, that you're doing the things that other people think are hard, then others will go, 'Wow, I wish I could be like that. What has she got that I haven't? What does he do that I still haven't tapped into and how do I achieve those results?' Leading by example and sharing freely who you are and what you stand for and what you believe in, sharing your successes along the way, will lead people to start following you.

I can't tell you how many times I have received a message from someone I have never heard of, yet they've been following my whole journey and they say, 'Oh I know what happened here and where you've been, all over the country and how your kids are growing up.' They know a lot about me. If you actually think about celebrities and how much people on the outside know about them, it's a similar thing within your world. Different levels of fame can be achieved in every industry, wherever people have similar interests.

If you really want to stand out, if you really want to get more bums on seats, building up your credibility, I guess your fame 'score' in your world is important and as that happens, bums on seats will become an easier and easier way to execute your events.

Some Negative Aspects of Having Raving Fans

I want to cover off a couple of negative aspects of raving fans that can occur so that you make sure you know what to do if something becomes a lot more difficult to handle.

First of all, those of you who think it takes a long time to build raving fans, yes it does. Fans need to be certain that you're a person who's here to stay and someone who's to be followed. You may also come across people who are a bit too clingy, if you like. They might intrude on your personal space. Or as people say, you might get a stalker.

Just ensure that all of the time you know what your boundaries are around people who you interact with within your community, how much you allow your clients to come into your life in your world, versus your friends and acquaintances and those people who you've just met a few times. Make sure that you have firm boundaries and that you know when to say no or when to really just call it as it is.

Then there's those people who perhaps come across as being fans, but you might start to get the sense that they're in for a free ride in terms of the things that you're doing. What I would always say in this situation is, number one, always check in with your gut. What's your gut telling you about this particular person? Is it that they want to get everything for free that you've actually got to offer? Or are they bringing into the relationship different value? Are they repaying you in a different way that perhaps you have not considered?

Are they always offering a hand to help and perhaps they come and help you prepare for an event or come earlier, to welcome guests? Are they repaying you in a different way? I think your gut will tell you exactly what is going on here, so I would listen to it strongly. In a similar sense those people who you may think are pushing the boundaries or are becoming a bit of a stalker, listen to your instincts.

Overall, having a raving fan or having multiple fans, which build over a period of time, is really a fantastic way to get those bums on seats. Make sure you ask them to promote your events that they will be more than happy to do. Just pick up the phone and ring them. Picking up the phone is always the most powerful way to get someone's commitment on something over sending a Facebook message or email and that way you guys can work out a strategy of how you can do it. Perhaps that way you can set up an affiliate structure or incentive in a way that if they help get a certain amount of people, a certain amount of dollars per ticket sold from their referrals, or perhaps if people end up doing a program that's bigger they also get that amount of money.

You have to work on it. If there's nothing to do here but show the best version of you and show those things you're achieving on the way then the raving fans will follow.

73

8. Scaling Up

Natasa Denman

*A*fter a certain period of time in business, once you have generated around $50,000-$100,000 in revenue over a 12-month period, it is recommended that you start looking at having a budget for paid advertising. More specifically, in this particular chapter we're going to talk about Facebook advertising. However, there are obviously ways to advertise through LinkedIn paid ads, Google AdWords and any banners on the Internet.

Most of the people reading this book would be looking at Facebook advertising, because it ends up being really targeted and you get a lot of awesome insights in terms of what your clients are responding to and you can test and measure it really well and then use that type of advertising in your promotions in other areas.

When Is Paid Advertising Right?

With paid advertising, what I realised specifically in my business is that with my warm network, my warm leads around me, I had exhausted them in terms of attending my events and referring to people who they knew. I needed to tap into fresh new people who didn't know me from a bar of soap, so that I would start building those fresh, new relationships from where I could build upon to a point where people knew me, liked me, trusted me. Then they are more likely to purchase whatever I'm offering at that particular event.

If you've been starting to factor 10-15 people into your events, you might see your numbers double or increase by a third, using paid advertising. I always treat paid advertising as the cherry on top.

I always do all of the other strategies I would normally do, in terms of the speaking gigs and reaching out and connecting to people in my current network, posting on social media, interacting with people that still doesn't cost me anything and relying on the paid advertising to be the cherry on top and not just completely letting it go.

I'm sure there will be a day where perhaps everything will be clicking over through paid advertising, but at this point in time, while writing this book, it is about utilising both of the avenues and ensuring that actually having people who know, like and trust you, be in your events.

It actually gives you more credibility and that following of raving fans that other people will respect. They might think, 'If those people trust her and like her, obviously it's safe to go there and do business with her.'

What starts to happen with paid advertising as well is that the pressure of doing it all yourself lessens, so you see bookings come through for your events and it just increases all the work you're doing.

When you turn up in the room and people also see you as a lot more professional, a well-established business. Obviously, if you're paying for advertising it means you're making money. A lot of people make that assumption.

And finally, paid advertising is amazing in terms of you discovering what your market responds to. That way you can filter that through to all your other marketing. So if something's working really well in paid advertising, you can change that copy on your website, you can change it in your offers that you're making, just through your free channels, your networking and your free speaking events.

Types of Paid Advertising

As I mentioned there are many different forms of paid advertising you can do and certainly another form is to become a sponsor of an event, which is something that I've only started to tackle. You pay for the rights to support an event and they mention you and it gives your brand a lot more exposure, which brings a lot more people to you.

Strategies for Paid Advertising

I want to share some strategies and tips and dos and don'ts around how to tackle paid advertising, because it can be risky. It can be scary. It can be like gambling away income that perhaps you're scared to risk, because perhaps your business may not be at a stage where it can afford to pay for advertising.

Let's go through the key three things you must consider and do around paid advertising.

1. You must find an expert. It is not a do-it-yourself task. Sometimes people think they can go to a Facebook ads course and learn how to do a little image and the copy and what to say in that and then create a landing page.

   I can tell you, you're going to waste so much time and money if you try to do this yourself. I know I did. I didn't go to a course, however, I did work it all out myself and watched YouTube videos and put stuff out there and really just spent hundreds of dollars without any click through or return on investment.

Finding an expert is crucial and that expert is obviously going to charge you a certain fee to run a certain ad campaign or like myself, I have got a permanent Facebook person on a monthly retainer. Now that I've been doing this for 18 months it works really well.

You decide on a certain budget for a particular event and if you're doing multiple events like myself, then you can set yourself a limit of spending $1,000 per event. On top of that, there are their management fees, because what they do is they adjust, they upload new images and they try different copy.

They also should have some kind of strategy on how to run your ads. Your Facebook support team should be someone that you work closely with and stay active in the process, as you know your business the best and to make the most of your investment this should be a closely monitored, tested and measured relationship.

When we started out we were advertising to get people straight to our event, which cost $49 to attend. In this particular time, because it was an event I was running in Sydney, and no one was booking.

I went back to my Facebook person and said, 'Look, can we do it a little bit differently? Is there a way that we can promote my actual book that is available in ebook and that way people will grab a whole copy of that 160-page book and they'll end up on our database?'

As the second step to this sequence, we would invite them to the event. If they don't come and they click out of it then they're still captured within our database and then perhaps within 6-8 months or a little bit down the track after we've built a relationship with them, they will come along to a future event. That way, not only are we getting people into our rooms, but we're building our database, which will ultimately result into more people coming into our rooms in future events.

We adjusted that and then a few months ago, our Facebook people started to use video in our ads and that captured a lot of attention and it was a positive strategy. Not all strategies are going to work. Some will work really well and some will be a flop and you'll need to adjust.

This is where you need to consider how much you're willing to risk and how far you want to take this, but once you find something that works really well, you know what they say, if you get given $5 for every $1 you spend, how many dollars are you going to spend?

That's how I look at advertising nowadays, I totally look at it as an investment and not a cost and that ultimately that will reap 10-20-30-fold, sometimes, return on investment.

2. You must be patient in the early months when you're starting paid advertising. What I have seen time and time again is people trial someone for 2, 3, 4 weeks even and they don't get a result.

    You know what? You may not get a result, possibly sometimes for 2-3 months, because your person needs to tweak, test and measure, adjust and certainly you need to be side by side with them and have very clear communication in terms of what's being trialled, what is being put out there, what are the percentages, conversion rates etc.

Practise patience because even I saw very minimal results early on. It was costing something like $80-$100 to get a person in my room, whereas nowadays it costs a lot less, it's down to about $20-$30.

When you look at the ticket price that was sold for $49, that kind of covers off all the advertising and the person is in there at the event, because your low cost events are not going to be a money making exercise.

The intention of these events is so people get to know you, meet you, see what value you've got to offer and then ultimately decide to work with you in your high-end programs.

Certainly when you are doing advertising you're asking for a lot lower risk, a lot lower cost to whatever you're advertising, or even you're offering something of value for free that's going to build your database and therefore those people are going to start to build that relationship with you.

3. The very last thing for paid advertising to consider is that you need to have your sequences and steps put into play.

If someone clicks on your ad, what is the first thing that's going to happen? What is the very next thing? Where are you going to invite them? What is it that you're going to offer them? What is this journey you're taking this lead on, who potentially becomes a prospect and then potentially becomes a client going to look like? Are there multiple steps or sequences?

Lately, our Facebook people, about a week before they actually start running events to our ad, they run some content. Some blogs to get people interested, to get people trusting us. Then when the ads hit, they start remarketing. Those people who have looked at and read that blog a week before, they get remarketed to, which means they get to see our ad, our ad follows them around Facebook and the Internet.

These are strategies that of course you can't learn and understand yourself if you're an expert at something completely different. That's why I suggest that you get someone else who has come highly recommended that you can work with closely.

The one thing to remember with this particular person is that you set goals together. Set goals as to what you like to achieve, where you want to see your events filled to, work backwards and forwards with them consistently and be proactive. I believe you're the best person, you're the one who cares the most about your business, and you're the one who's investing the money.

81

You must be proactive in terms of how you treat the relationship and that you play that patience card in the early days. If you are going to be impatient, if you jump from one provider to another provider, which I have also seen happen in the past, then what's going to happen is that you're going to get mixed results.

But also every time you're restarting you're letting go and throwing away that money you've invested in beforehand, because these guys collect data, they know what certain people are responding to and they're keeping an eye out.

Once they've got the formula pretty close they can then replicate it time and time again and then it's about you just turning up, doing your events and achieving the success you've already dreamed of.

Create a Giveaway to Go With Your Paid Advertising

A very hot tip that I want to share with you in this particular chapter about paid advertising is to find something that you can give away before selling something else. This can be a book if you've written a book, an ebook or a checklist, or a template for some-thing. That way your database will be built and you can stay in touch with these people regularly, so that potentially in the future they become a client of yours. When I give away my *Ultimate 48 Hour Author* book, its full version as an ebook, I get extraordinary conversion of 65% regularly. That is a huge list-building tool and people love the massive value they receive.

Fears Around Paid Advertising

Then there's a lot of fear around paid advertising and the fear is, what if you waste a lot of money, in this case, and you get no results? What I say is if you are not willing to part with that money, if you cannot take the worst case scenario, then you are not ready to do paid advertising. You must be willing to take the risk and be able to part with the money and if you're willing to take the risk and say, I'm going to do this and it may not work out, then it's time to do it.

If it's too scary, if you can't put food on the table because you've put this money into paid advertising, it is not the right time to start. Just consider that, and that is why at the beginning of the chapter I said that if your business is turning over $50,000-$100,000 a year and you're starting to run out of those warm leads in your network, it's time to step it up.

Learning About Paid Advertising

Some of you may want to still consider going to a course and learning how to do it yourselves. My recommendation is not to, because you don't want to dilute what your core expertise is. Learning a new skill will take time. Your efforts are best put towards more sales and marketing, in other words what you actually provide. Your expertise is in actually going deeper, rather than learning a whole other skill that can take a good year or two to master.

The Right Time. When is the Right Time?

We said that earlier. The right time is when you're comfortable in taking this leap to the paid advertising world. Otherwise if you're not ready to take the leap of faith, if you're not ready to part with some money that's going to be spent on the testing and measuring, then it's not the right time.

Ultimately, paid advertising can get your business to start to scale. Where it might have been in an infancy stage and you've grown, now it's time to scale and that's where your events can get quite big and successful. Another form of paid advertising is sponsorships. The way to making a sponsorship successful for you is to decide before you invest in it, what is the outcome that you want as a result.

This year I've invested in three types of sponsorships. The outcome is that I will have 10 authors for each of my 48-hour author retreats. This will take 12-months to eventuate and at the end of those 12 months I'll know whether those sponsorships were worthwhile and that it was a well invested strategy.

But again, investing in a sponsorship, I'm willing to take the risk and say, 'Look, I'm going to pay out whatever it is asked for and be willing to accept the fact that I may not get anything out of this.' Certainly I will do my best and the aim is to work with it and submit whatever I need to submit to the sponsor, to the people that I'm sponsoring and make sure I follow up and ask for as many opportunities as possible with them and if nothing eventuates out of it, then I'd also be willing to walk away and take that as feedback.

Well done, go out there, give it a go, and hire an expert if the time is ready for you. If not, wait till you're ready and then you'll know exactly what to do when you start your paid advertising campaigns.

Part 2

Prepare

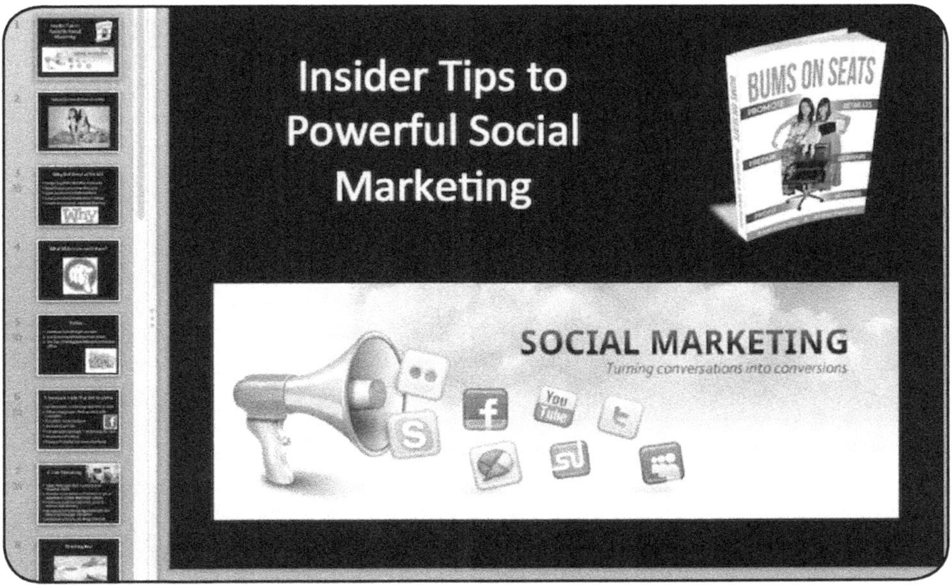

9. Easy Done

Francesca Moi

Sometimes you'll wish you could clone yourself if you don't work on your systems! I have been there and being disorganised can be really painful and it's not good for your business.

Having everything organised for an event, before, during, after, having everyone knowing what to do at the event is absolutely a must. I am very spontaneous and I was struggling at the beginning with the logistics. Being creative I was procrastinating on creating checklists and things like that because I used to see them as a waste of time. Oh lord! I wish I could go back in time and tell that Francesca that CHECKLISTS and SYSTEMS are the foundations in business.

I just didn't like to organise everything and put systems in place. In my brain I just knew how the event was going to run and I thought that common sense would be common. What I realised along the way is that the bigger the event becomes, the harder it is to have your team organised and to have the crew on the same page.

I did have to put in place a list of things to do and things not to forget to bring to the event and what to do and how to set up the room and what to expect from the volunteers on the night. Every single time we do an event I do a briefing with them to ensure everyone knows what they have to do and when.

Logistics, even if you are like me, a very spontaneous person who doesn't like systems, they are actually a must. It is actually key to running a successful event. The bigger the event becomes, the more things you have to remember to bring along with you. The bigger the night is, if you are the presenter like I am and have been, it becomes very full on.

You're trying to do everything that you want to do, you're trying to remember to mention everything you had the intention to tell your attendees, to remind everyone of everything, but then sometimes, you're not a machine. Things happen, clients start to ask you questions, you're on stage and you can see the girls in the background doing things and getting everything ready for you and you can easily forget something if you don't have a checklist. You might forget to tell them something that's really important.

As I mentioned in Chapter 2, one of my biggest tips to put bums on seats is to invite the attendees of one event to come along to the next event offering them a super discount price if they book straight away. A couple of times I forgot to do that on stage because I didn't have a checklist with me and neither did my team. That mistake cost us a lot of money and we missed out on a fully booked event next time.

Using a Checklist as a Key Part of Your Logistics

Having a checklist of things to say on the night, a checklist of things to do before the event, what to bring to the event, what to do at the event and what to do after the event, they are a must.

It will save you from forgetting important things; it will make your life and your assistant's life easier. I can promise you that, since we've had checklists in place. It will be easy to organise volunteers and crewmembers. Also for the venue it's a lot easier, if you've got a checklist of things that need to be in the room for you for your next event. The venue will find it a lot easier as well. You'll be less stressed and it will be easier to run the event and it will be quicker to set up the event and to run it. It's a no brainer.

I can promise you that I've done it before without checklists and since we've got a checklist in place everything is so much smoother, more professional and super organised and relaxed.

This will also avoid making huge mistakes and looking unprofessional. You might have people lining up to come to your events and it doesn't look good to see that there's a lot of people waiting, and your crew running around not knowing what to do. It's not what you want as a first impression, remember the first 5 seconds are key to give them an idea on what to expect on the night.

CHECK LIST 1:
To Do Days Prior Meetup:

- ☐ *Ice breaker game*
- ☐ *Your short presentation*
- ☐ *Promote on Facebook*
- ☐ *Do a live Periscope*
- ☐ *Send a message to people asking if they are coming along*
- ☐ *Check tickets are still available*
- ☐ *Promote it*
- ☐ *Cross promote it*
- ☐ *Post on Meetup Mafia Group.*

To Print:
- ☐ *Name Tags from Meetup for Lucky Draw*
- ☐ *Attendee List (from Meetup or cross promotion file)*
- ☐ *Labels on label paper*
- ☐ *Lucky draw prize.*

What Is Logistics When It Comes to Events?

What I mean by logistics is exactly, literally, what to do before, during and after your event. How to organise yourself, what to bring, what to do at the event, who does what, what to pack and how.

The first checklist that I suggest you create is the promotion checklist, how to promote the same event on multiple Social Media, e.g.:

- *Meetup*
- *Facebook,*
- *and Eventbrite.*

Ensure that you promote it on your Facebook groups and you create an event on Facebook, you don't just advertise it.

You do webinars promoting that event and you do podcasts.

You go and speak at other events, inviting people to your event.

If you don't write all these ideas on how to promote it down, you will only do a couple of them and then you will wonder why you don't have many people attending your event.

There are a lot of steps you need to take to ensure that you get people to your event. The super important things to remember are the prizes, the lucky draws. What prizes are you going to give on the night? You have to organise that on time, make sure you ask on social media for people to offer prizes for you.

That is actually another great way to "promote" your event, by asking for prizes to other business owners.

The speakers, how are you going to choose the speakers? You've got to lock them in.

The more advanced your events become the more you will get a higher level of quality speakers. Book your speaker in. It will look so professional when another speaker asks to speak and you say, 'We have speakers scheduled until June next year.'

BOOM! ☺

Perception to the roof.

Remember it's all about perception. Once you are perceived as successful that means you are going to start to monetise things very soon. So don't give up now, keep working on it!

Go to the appendices for checklists that Natasa and I use for our events. You can check them out; pick the ones you like, change them, tweak them, but make sure you follow step-by-step what we suggest you do.

In the appendices there are few different checklists. One of them is what to do before the event, how to promote the event, what to do during the event and what to do after.

Once you've finished the event it's not finished and there's a lot of things you need to do and a lot of follow up for your clients to make sure they've had an amazing, outstanding experience.

The Purpose of Exceptional Logistics

The goal of all these logistics, of running an event, is to wow your people, to give them more than enough value.

You want to give them so much knowledge and value that they're going to love you, talk about you to all your friends and your community, bringing more people to the next event and helping you create that credibility to position yourself as a person of influence in your field.

Some things that I've done and still do nowadays are to have a page for my assistant and for myself.

It's called the 'aha moments' page.

On the left hand side of a notepad, we will put all the things we've done wrong and can improve on and on the right hand side all the things we've done well and have actually worked.

Even if they're not in the checklist they're going to go in there, because they're going to go in the next checklist.

It's a powerful way to learn and improve the events, so every time I look at my assistant I can tell her, wrong or right and she will write down at that point, 'You told me there was something wrong when you were speaking about this subject ***, what was it?'

Then of course we have a meeting after the event, straight away, and say, 'When I told you 'wrong', I was talking about that, it was because I shouldn't have said that.' When I say, 'Oh yeah, yeah, I made that joke about whatever and everyone laughed and that created that beautiful environment in the room, so I'd do something like that again.'

So we actually improve my speech, and the event by writing it all down and learn from mistakes and from wins.

I am still spontaneous, on stage, I don't want to become a robot on stage nor do I want you to become fake on stage, but sometimes when you are on stage you have been trying to say something the right way for a while and all of a sudden it happens, you want to remember how you said it so you can become a pro at running events and at public speaking by engaging with your audience.

| | Home | Insert | Page Layout | Formulas | Data | Review | View |

D4

	A	B	C	D	E
1	**Name**	**Surname**	**Number Of RSVP**	**Paid**	**Arrived**
2					
3	Adrian	Hanks	1		
4	Ashok	Kumar	1		
5	Cheryl	Franklin	1		
6	David	Kaity	1		
7	David	Long	1		
8	Deborah	Mitchel	1		
9	Dimitri	Taylor	1		
10	Dianne	Armbrust	1		
11	Di	Ayling	2		
12					
13	Elizabeth	Cronje	1		
14	Floyd	Collins	1		
15	Gabrielle	Olga	1		
16	Jane	Manson	0	Cancelled	
17	Jane	Webster	1		
18	John	C	2		
19					
20	Julie		2		
21					
22	Jamie	Rose	1		
23	Karen	Meissner	1		
24	Karen	McCauley	1		
25	Lalande	Foote	1		
26	Leonie	Campbell	1		
27	Megan	Gibson	2		
28					
29	Marc	Newman	1		
30	Maree	Elyse-Thomas	1		
31	Mario	Bono	1		
32	Michael	Cassidy	1		
33	Naomi	Smith	1		
34	Petra	Williams	1		YES
35	Raewyn	Mai	1		
36	Rebecca	Nicholls	1		
37	Sandra	Mayne	1		
38	Tom	Walden	1		
39	Tony	Nicklason	1		
40			36		

Ensuring Attendance with Checklists

One of the fears for many people is that they've got a checklist, everything is done, but what if they don't have the number of attendees that they wanted? That's part of the checklist, to make sure that you've got the numbers as you go.

For example, every time I have an event that's got 10 days until the event I'm going to ensure that: 'Okay, how many tickets did we want to sell? How many did we sell? From here to there we're going to sell at least five tickets a day.' Your entire team is going to work towards selling five tickets a day and if you've put in the intention and you're doing it the right way, it is going to happen. Facebook is really powerful for those things.

Get Your Venue Sorted

How to find the venue is one of the questions a lot of the clients ask me very often. I've just been in Sydney for a business trip. When I was there I went out and about to different pubs and different hotels and venues, function rooms, where they hire function rooms and I checked them out. You just take your little taxi and you go around, check them out and try to make a deal with the manager. You go there with your whole year scheduled with all your events and you go to the venue.

It's so powerful, you say, 'Look, these are the events that I'm doing this year. There's an event every 10 days and there's four workshops a year and this is what I do. I'm looking for one venue to stick to so it's easy for us. We've got free parking, all the facilities we're looking for, are you happy with me? We're happy with you.' And you commit. That's the best way to get a really huge discount with the venues and it's easier for you, you have peace of mind, you've booked all your dates, it's done, you're not going to procrastinate, you're not going to let one date slip.

It's all in there, you've done it, it's promoted, boom.

You can do the same with the venues, the guest speakers, the lucky draw to give on the night, you just want to have the whole year planned in advance so you know what speaker you're getting when and what the dates are, you've got the venue booked, everything is done for you so you don't have to stress. 'Oh my god, I've got an event in 10 days and I haven't got a guest speaker yet.' You want everything to be booked and done so you don't have to worry about it and you don't have to stress.

The checklist is going to help you not forget stuff. A couple of times it happened to me, before I had checklists in place, I did forget things that were really important, like the posters or the banner, which just would make the room warmer and creates that environment. If you do forget something, what I suggest you do is to double-check the checklist before you leave your office and go to the event. Usually for cables and things like that I have two spare ones all the time, so if I do misplace one or can't find one we always manage to have a backup.

My favourite checklist of all is the 'what to print before the event list'. I always struggled to remember to print everything at office works and then I used to find myself printing from my home printer last minute. Have a checklist of forms you need to have on the night, posters, flyers, name tags, attendee lists and start printing a couple of days before the event. So that you won't have to panic last minute to print.

Now we're going to go into the three actions to take:

1) Get the checklist, read them out and make sure you use the ones that are appropriate for your events.

2) Choose the dates for your 12 months and pick the venue and the topics and the guest speakers and the lucky draws. Get on it, do the plan; you've got it all.

3) Send the email out. You've got a template email that you can

use, the same one for everyone. 'I'd love to have you at my next event, these are the dates.' And I'll send it to all my speakers. I hope you can choose a date and we'd love to have you as a guest speaker at our events.

These are some actions you can take. Logistics is key. Enjoy and make sure that you're super organised so your people are going to enjoy you too.

10. Famous Clicker

Natasa Denman

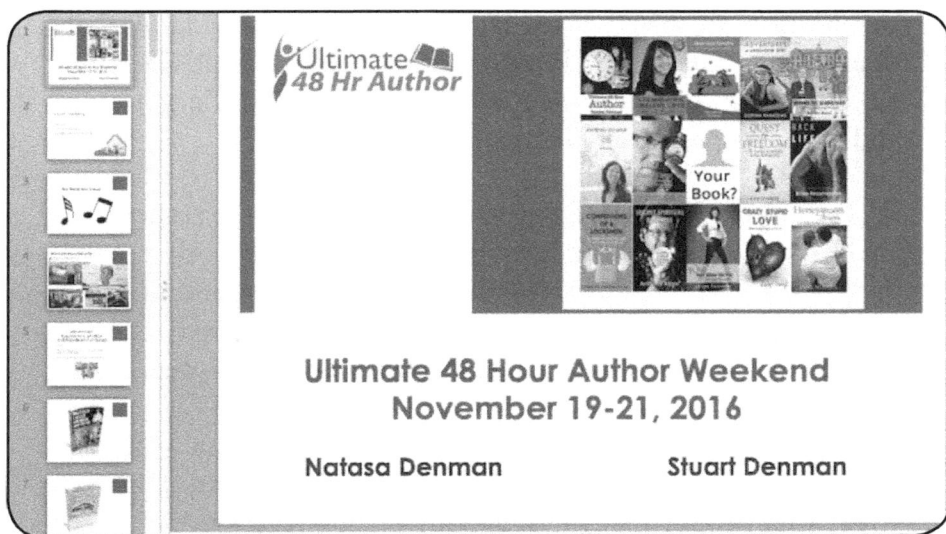

There is a very popular saying out there, 'Death by PowerPoint.' If you were to take this on as a truth, then you shouldn't have any PowerPoint presentations in any of your events.

However, according to *The Index of Learning Styles*, by Dr Richard Feldman and Barbara Soloman, 65% of the human population are visual learners? In knowing that, addressing that and having learning tools, like a PowerPoint, it can be very powerful in engaging your audience at your event.

A good PowerPoint can be a driver to elicit emotional responses. By sharing images or videos throughout your presentation and if you keep your words on your PowerPoint to a minimum. Just use it as a guide to help you get through the presentation as well as engage the audience, then you won't have the case of 'Death by PowerPoint'.

Having a presentation and those visual cues for people really makes you look a lot more professional and it assists in the learning success of those who attend your events.

In addition to visual learners, it's good to understand that there's also auditory and kinaesthetic learning as well. Catering for every type of learner is a recommended way of organising and preparing for your events.

With auditory learners, using sound through your presentation, anchoring songs, perhaps having a song as people work in or as part of a specific break, having that song again, something that's a theme song around what you do will get people excited and will also get people to remember every time they hear that song.

With kinaesthetic learners perhaps it's best that you use handouts and give them something to touch or feel and interact with other people. Get them moving during your events.

How to Create PowerPoint Presentations

In this particular chapter we will focus more on how to create a PowerPoint and what are important aspects of it and in which order to present your workshop or your event, so that you can monetise it and get people to invest further with you for that transformative experience you're offering.

PowerPoints are really great for keeping you on track, especially in the early days, when you're perhaps not as confident as a speaker and a presenter. It will keep you on track in terms of what point you're trying to make and you can have visual cues for yourself.

As I said, less is more. With PowerPoints just use less words, really just key words and then elaborate on those. This is really important, however I do understand that if earlier in your journey of running events you are using more words, then expect that you will refine that. Nowadays I really just put one or two words on a slide with an image that corresponds with what I'm trying to say and this keeps people having something to look at. This also keeps me on track of where I am in the presentation so I know where I can time things in the appropriate manner; depending on how much time I've been allocated.

People love taking notes and usually when they ask you to please send through the PowerPoint after a presentation that means they've seen a lot of value in what you've got to offer and that's something they may want to refer to in future times.

101

There are a few different platforms that you can use to create your visual presentation and Microsoft PowerPoint is not the only one. If you are a Mac user they have the software called Keynote for Apple products. As well as this there's an online software that you can invest in that's called Prezi and that really brings your visual presentations to life and makes them a lot more interactive with the audience and a little bit more sophisticated.

I've always used PowerPoint. I know how to use it well, I know how to do it very quickly and that's what I choose to continue using. I have had a go at using Keynote and that was also very similar to use and had some components that were missing within PowerPoint so sometimes I could switch from one to the other if need be.

What I also want you to be very mindful of is to be careful if techie issues arise, is to have your backup plans in case your

PowerPoint won't play. Perhaps have your slides printed out and taken with you so if you don't have a PowerPoint then you can still have those guiding points just in your hands. Do this, engage your audience and just do your presentation.

How Long Does it Take to Create a PowerPoint Presentation?

Take your time and learn how to use PowerPoint. There are a lot of videos on YouTube you can access to learn the basics. It is well worth investing time, because if you're going to do regular events you're going to continuously have to do PowerPoint presentations and after a while what will happen is that you will have so many presentations that you can cut and paste a lot of your slides and combine them to create new ones.

The initial starting point is where you're going to spend the most time and after a while you should be able to tap into the other presentations and at this point in time it takes me about 10-30 minutes to prepare a 1-hour webinar presentation or a 1-hour workshop.

Certainly it would take a couple of hours to pull it all together if it's a full day or a two-day event. However, that's not long knowing how I would be using that multiple times in the future and it's always the first time that it takes the longest. The next time you might just refine the starting or the finishing slides.

Learn how to troubleshoot it and always have backups in terms of what you'll do if certain things don't happen or they don't play out. After a while I trust you'll have the confidence to run your event and know your stuff so well you don't need the PowerPoint presentation and sometimes I choose not to have anything, if they're short presentations. Learn to practice not being as reliant on them.

The Key Components of PowerPoints

Let's go through some key components that your PowerPoint needs to contain to really take your attendees on a journey and an experience that they love so much they want to do further work with you.

I want you to talk about your story. The journey of your zero to hero story is a component that I always like to start off with in my presentations, because a lot of times you'll stand up in front of people who can't tell you from a bar of soap. Telling your story and going through the ups and downs of what happened in your life is important because people want to see an aspect in you that they want for themselves.

If they can see that where you started is perhaps where they are right now (and we tend to attract people who are X amount of steps before where we have arrived), it's really important to share that particular story. Use some visuals and take them through the positive and perhaps negative aspects of how you have attained the success you've attained and what you're trying to teach them.

Start off with that, get them interacting and engaging and perhaps getting them to give you back the learnings that they've received from listening to your zero to hero story. This is a great way to build rapport and for them to see that what you are today wasn't always that way and that there was a journey of trials and tribulations that you had to go through.

Once you have gone through the story it's really great to give people the outcomes of what you will teach them on that particular date or at that particular event. I call that the 'what' slide, so I use what I call format in my presentations. I learnt this in coaching school and that is sharing the 'why', the 'what', the 'how' and then the 'what if'. If you notice throughout the chapters throughout this book, that's the exact same format we have been delivering this information to you in.

103

Initially when we start out we're talking about all the benefits as to why you need to know something. When you started off this chapter, talking about why PowerPoint was so important, what the benefits of it are, we talked about the visual learners, we talked about making it look professional, eliciting emotional responses and keeping you on track. Those are all benefits on why it's important to do a PowerPoint presentation at your events.

Then in the 'what' I talked about what kind of presentations to do visually. We talked about PowerPoint, Keynote and Prezi. As well as that I wanted to teach you the three key things that you needed to know about creating a successful PowerPoint presentation.

Now into the 'how'. Now I'm giving you different tips and tricks and delving a bit deeper into each point, so I can explain it and at the end as I finish off the 'how' section we're going to go into the 'what if'. The 'what if' is really a section where you ask the audience, 'Are there any questions?'

Usually there are objections or people who want to challenge you around a specific point that you've been covering in that section. After every section of the presentation, if you're doing three major points, then what you want to do is stop after each point and ask if the audience has any questions. A really great way to do this is to ask them, 'What did you learn?' 'What did you notice?' And 'what do you want to share?' These are three questions you can ask them rather than saying, 'Has anyone got any questions.'

That's something that I also learnt in other workshops that I attended and it was really great, because it gets people to actually think more about what they learnt and noticed. It gets people sharing more. When you ask them directly if they've got any questions, it's a little bit more of a closed off way to ask for interaction.

At the beginning of a presentation, when you're doing the 'why', there's a great trick you can do to get the audience to talk amongst themselves. Before you start your story, you could say, 'Okay, I want you to form groups of 2-3 people and talk to each other about why you are here today, what you'd like to learn and depending on what your topic is, what's your biggest challenge around this particular topic and then what would happen if you did nothing about it.'

Obviously they're in the room wanting to solve a particular pain, having a particular problem or wanting to achieve a specific result. Ask them that and get them into groups of 2-3 people and it works really well to build up that 'why'. Then note down those points on a whiteboard.

Then you don't have to give them the benefits, the whole room comes up with the benefits on your behalf and if there's something that they've missed or you want to add on for them, certainly you can do it with them. That's a great way to begin the day with an interaction and you can make it all about them before you go into your story.

Tweaking Your Presentations Regularly

Okay, so a hot tip around running/having PowerPoints is to make sure that you're adjusting and refining them regularly, so they're current to the results that you're reporting, to your story, to different insights that you've had as you've been running your events. It's especially true if you're doing one event over and over throughout the year. You want to keep adjusting it and making it more current to the version of you that is now.

Using Visuals in Your Presentations

The last tip around PowerPoints is making sure that you use one image on every single slide and perhaps a video once or twice throughout the presentation, just to get people to break their state and take a journey.

A video's a great way of taking them on a journey, experiencing what something is and actually sharing and making a really great point. You can Google a lot of different images and look up videos on YouTube that you can play for your audience. This is really great, because having something to look at helps them tremendously. Make sure you use pictures and videos that are not copyrighted.

A picture says a thousand words and my rule is that I always have at least one image on each of my slides, so that my audience doesn't experience only words, words, words, after which they really do end up walking away feeling that they've had that death by PowerPoint experience.

What Are Some Objections Against Using PowerPoints?

As we've gone through the 'how' now, this is where I can cover off the 'what if' section. If you were writing a program or a product or a book such as this, we can go into the 'what if'. In my notes I'll write down, what the kinds of questions are an audience would ask me. Here I've written down a few.

'I don't know how to create it, it takes time to learn this stuff'. That would be an objection by someone who is in the audience. I would tell them, 'I think it's worthwhile to take the time to learn how to do visual presentations, because it's a great way not to be waiting on someone else to do it for you and to change things up as you feel you need to.'

I had a client who is over 70, whom I showed how to use Keynote. She had a bit of a play, we did it together and then I let her have a bit of a go on her own and she did it and felt so empowered to be able to do it, because she knew that anywhere she went, she could be seen as a professional speaker who brought great value to the audience and that it really doesn't take all that long. It's really about knowing a few basics that could enhance everything that you do.

Other people may be scared about having that 'techie' failure that I suggested earlier. Have all your slides printed out for your reference, so if you do have all techie equipment that lets you down on the night, you've got your guiding presentation to share what you need to share with the audience. That way you can overcome that and pretend like it was always planned as it was.

Last of all, if you're worried that your PowerPoint is too much, or whether people are going to walk away feeling like they've had 'Death by PowerPoint', what I always say is to use the principle of 'less is more'. Get someone else to have a look at your presentation, use more visuals and those prompters or videos, so that way people really get immersed in what you're delivering.

I trust this has given you a few tips around how to create it, especially using format and structuring in the 'why', 'what', 'how', 'what if' manner so that your audience also gets catered for. Earlier in the chapter we said that there's visual, kinaesthetic and auditory learners. In addition to this, there are also people who are more 'why' inclined, so 'why the hell should I know this?' There's the 'what' people, definitely a lot of 'how' people, 'just tell me how to do it'. And then there's the people who always put their hand up and go, 'what if this' and 'what if that'.

All the best and go out and get your first presentation created!

Part 3

Profit

109

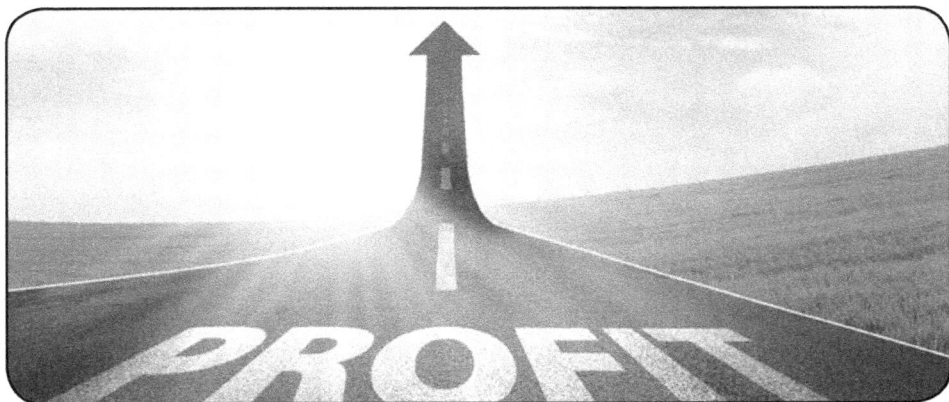

Our Sponsors

Key Person of Influence
KPI will be giving us away free books

Empowering Events
Offers discounted tickets to events, seminars and workshops.

Point TV
Discounts to attend TV Shows

Add a Sponsor →

11. Sponsor Power

Francesca Moi

Would it be great if you could find a sponsor to pay and cover the cost of your events, or of the venue, or of the canapés, nibbles, prizes, books to give away on the night? Wouldn't that be cool?

I know, right? And the thing is, a lot of people will think who am I to get sponsored? My event is too small, or I'm not someone who will be sponsored. I guarantee you, that's not true. Everyone can get sponsors and it's very easy to do, so you just have to find a way to do it.

I have to say that I thought exactly the same as you, and it took me 8 months to start getting sponsors for my events because I thought my 50 people per event were not enough. But I can guarantee you even 10 people per event are enough to get a small business interested in sponsoring your groups and your events.

Getting a sponsor is not just about money it's about credibility. If you imagine you promote your event and you say, 'I'm so excited to let you know that we've got three sponsors for the next event and they're going to cover the cost of the canapés and drinks for all of you. Make sure you come along to this event for $120 and we'll get these amazing sponsors.'

The bigger the company that will sponsor you the better it is and the more credibility that you're going to get. The more numbers of sponsors you get; the more credibility you'll have.

You'll have less stress at that event. A lot of the times people are afraid to run events as they're afraid they won't be able to cover costs. If you do find a sponsor it's going to help you to cover costs. Don't stress about getting the right number. The right number will come along anyway but without stress, which is very good.

Sponsors Add Value to Your Events

It's going to add a lot of value to the event. The more reason why people will come along to this event, because they're only spending $20 or $10 or whatever the price you want to put it as – $40 and they're getting food, they're getting a better venue, they're getting drinks, they're getting better quality prizes. They can get more; it's an incentive for them. They'll want to go to your event.

Having sponsors is also going to help you grow your network, as it's more likely the sponsor will promote that event for you in their database. It's a win-win situation. More bums on seats for you. You're going to be able to use their name to promote your events. If you've got a big sponsor that's famous in your target market, then you're definitely going to get more people's attention when you're promoting the event.

Also it's another great way to remind people about your event and to attract attention when you post on social medias. 'Looking for sponsors for our next event', DATE and LINK ☺ BOOM all of a sudden there is something in it for them and people are going to start to tag successful business owners that are looking to sponsor others. It's a great way to promote your event!

Sponsorships Create Win-Win Situations

Why do businesses enjoy being a sponsor? Why do companies want to help your event? It's because you might have the same target market attending the event and they are going to love the advertisement you are going to do for them. They're going to get promotions and a bigger market and you're going to get your events sponsored. It's a win-win situation for everyone.

That's how Natasa and I roll. We love to create win-win situations for everyone.

Finding the Right Sponsors

How are we going to do this? How are we going to find someone to sponsor us?

You're going to choose, first of all, the sponsors that have a name and that will add credibility to your event. I'm going to give you a little example here. I do events for business owners and entrepreneurs. A great sponsor for me would be something like Office Works, or a printer, or any big company. Through them you'll be able to get more credibility. If we want to start with a smaller company then I could ask other business coaches, or people who sell products to have a trading table at my events. For example, I've had a lady from Arbonne at my events apart from other companies too.

If you are in fitness and you're a personal trainer, you could get a gym sponsoring you. How are you going to do that? Okay, so I'm going to tell you this right now. Search for the sponsors that are constantly sponsoring other events and other Meetups in your area or in Australia. Have a look at who's sponsoring who and contact the head office and ask them to sponsor your events. The bigger the numbers of your Meetup group, or of past attendees of your events, the better chances you have to get a big company to sponsor you.

113

You can start small; you can start local. You can go to the local printer and say, 'Look, I'm running this event, we need the budget to print a banner. Would you be able to please promote us and we'll put a logo of your business on the banner and in the Meetup when we advertise the events?' It's really about creating a win-win situation. The magic thing about sponsoring is that as soon as you start to get some sponsors, then the other ones will contact you. The other businesses and companies will contact you. 'We want to sponsor your event, how are we going to do that?' It's about getting it started. It's all about creating credibility and perception.

The First Sponsors Are the Hardest to Get

If you've never had any sponsors, the first one will be the toughest one to get. But once you've got some sponsors, once you've grown that credibility already, then that's when you're going to get seen and you're going to attract more sponsors as well.

What if you can't find anyone? Well, to be honest I've never found someone that has not found a sponsor. You can lower the price in the beginning and what I did in one of my events, I said, 'You know you can put a trading table in my event and just give me $200 and you'll make the money back on the night for sure.'

It depends on the number you get for the night and you can even charge $20 for a trading table. If you get 3 sponsors at $60 you can buy some drinks for the people. Be smart, start low and grow your credibility and as you grow, the higher you get, the chances are you're going to get to be sponsored.

Sometimes we are running our business in fear, people will tell us we're afraid we're going to fail, we're afraid of being declined or being rejected. What I can tell you is that you'll just have to start thinking big. Stop thinking small and local. Just go to the big companies, go to Upwork, go to a company where they're looking to expand and reach more people in Australia. Go to those companies and tell them that you can help them. Start from a place of, 'I have something powerful that you need and we can create a win-win situation for everyone.'

I also find that networking is always the best way to meet new sponsors. Just the other day I attended an Italian Chamber of Commerce event and one of the sponsors was an Italian gentleman who started importing Italian wine. Being Italian I was very excited about trying the wine, and I found it absolutely delicious. So straight away I mentioned to him about providing some bottles as a lucky draw prize and from there we start to create a collaboration.

My clients loved the wine and I invited his company to sponsor my events. It's really easy to find sponsors if you keep your eyes open ☺

Why Do Companies Do Sponsorships?

Why would a sponsor listen to you when you've got a small community? Again, because this is how the world is changing now. Advertising is not just creating an ad and putting it on Facebook, or putting it on TV or radio, advertising is about being seen. The more you're seen the more you're going to get visitors to your website. The more you're seen, the more you put your name out there, the more you're going to get followers and clients.

Every big company knows that they have to be out there, that they have to expand to be able to grow their business.

Your group is going to grow exponentially and they can get on board now when it's not too big and you can guarantee them the cheapest possible price for the next 12 months.

You are the one in charge, you're the one who believes your

community is going to become huge and you're doing them a favour and it's not them doing you a favour. It depends on how you package or how you present the things to them as well. If you go and beg them to be your sponsor, they're going to go, 'Hmm, I'm not sure I really want to sponsor you, because it looks like you're not successful yet.'

But if you place it properly, if you do it the right way, then they are definitely going to see the value in it. It's about you, how you frame your speech, how you frame your negotiation.

Maybe then one of the things you'll want to do is to learn how to negotiate. It can be really powerful.

What About You Start to be a Sponsor of Other Events?

Natasa has done this in 2016 with very large companies. It's a very powerful way to tap into a new market and a cold audience. Natasa's deals are around speaking, so she agrees to be a paid sponsor for them and ensure that they will let her speak at their events at least twice a year.

I have been sponsoring smaller local groups and networking events and I am finding huge benefits from it.

Okay, so three steps you're going to get from this chapter are:

1. Look out for sponsors and big companies that your target market would like to buy from. If you're a business owner and you're a business coach then look out for things that people would like for the office and that people would need for organisation, planners and books and things that your clients would need and that add value and make you an expert.

2. Start to write sponsorship letters so that you are ready to approach companies when you find one. When you

find someone who you really want to sponsor you, you don't have to take too much time to contact them. You just go home, get that email out that's a template, boom, you send it, all done and you don't have to think about it any more. Very powerful and not time consuming at all.

3. When you go to other successful events you can see the marketing so you can see how they've promoted it, you can see their sponsors. Look out and go and approach their sponsors as well. Big companies that sponsor don't want to sponsor one event or one Meetup. The ones they want are the ones where they see the benefit; they're going to start to promote more and more Meetup groups and events.

Get out there, grow your network, expand, think big and make it happen!

12. TOP Dollar

Natasa Denman

High End Programs

Running events is an art form. Selling people into your high-end events and programs is an absolute skill that needs to be mastered. Having the right high-end program is key to your success and to you having a sustainable and profitable business.

Your high-end events are really where your clients get to experience that true immersion and transformation where their lives start to take a different trajectory to success and a better way of living and creating their dream lifestyle.

They get to truly experience the value that you've got to deliver and go deep with you.

In your introductory events such as speaking gigs, half-day events or even full-day events, they may get the surface-level stuff.

They may be working with you so they can go into some depth, but the particular details are where they get to find out how to truly model what you've created for yourself, so that they can do it exactly the same way for themselves.

Your High-End Events Are Where You Go Deep

In this particular book, for example, we're giving you a lot of tips and strategies. There's so much more depth in all of these that if we were to sit down with you and spend a few days with you, that's where we would be able to really show you the depth and the smaller steps within each of the strategies that we're sharing here.

There's only so much that we could share and say within a book. Otherwise you'd be sitting and reading this book for months on end.

Frankly, the human mind likes things to be delivered easy and simple and to have that experiential learning. The value is in the experience, when we're talking about high-end programs.

How can you create an unforgettable, transformative and life changing experience for your clients? How can you create an experience that's going to really differentiate you from the competitors and make you the go-to person for having that particular problem solved?

Ultimately, high-end programs, make your business highly profitable and really leveraged, so that you only need to have yourself and perhaps a few support people to sustain and run a 7-figure business, such as we do.

It creates the opportunity for people to get a real VIP experience, or quite exclusive and get those clients to go deep with you. This is the reward.

I call it the icing on the cake, because everything that you do to get bums on seats, into your low-cost events, to get those speaking gigs, leads to the true reward.

The outcome of all the hard work that you do, like we do for all the Ultimate 48-Hour Authors, is to discover them, to get them to commit to the program, and to get them to have the experience that goes deep.

Executing those retreats is where the reward is for building those relationships. Doing all that speaking and those low-cost events, it comes to a climax at that high-end program.

Many people tend to see the end result on Social Media, about us running a retreat and say, 'Oh wow, I want to do that.'

However, doing that involves everything that you're learning through this book. A high-end program is the execution of all that work that has culminated to come to that point.

If you're charging $5,000-$10,000-$15,000, whatever amount it is for your high-end program, just realise that you're not just getting paid for that weekend.

You also need to take into consideration all the work that you've done prior to that and how much effort you put in and how much marketing or advertising you've done to make it a profitable business.

After all, just because it's the one weekend where people are paying whatever amount it is to work with you and you walk away with a 6-figure turnover that weekend, it's not just that weekend. Look at it as an overall year, an overall number of months.

If you don't focus on creating a high-end program or a high-end experience, then you'll need to go through a massive volume to create that turnover.

You won't be leveraged, you won't build your business much beyond 6 figures and realistically your clients might be only getting a little taste of you, rather than the transformational experience that you can offer in a real immersion program.

How to Build That Experience of a High-End Program

What I want to talk to you about in this chapter is how to build that experience as your high-end.

What kind of inclusions you should put in it? How do you fill it and how can people walk away with some of those tangible outcomes that you can offer?

If they have something to walk away with (our authors walk away with a book at the end of their experience with us), that's something that they'll remember forever and they've got something to show for it as well.

It's not always possible for service-based businesses to do that, but you can still get creative.

You can always turn something intangible into something tangible that people can have at the end of their experience.

Where do you start?

You start with a table of value.

I always say to people, you never, ever create anything until you've sold it and that table of value (you'll see an example of at the back of this book) would include all the tangible and the intangible items.

By doing that and obviously putting what the value and the investment of the various components is, people can see that they can walk away with so much value if they spend this weekend or this amount of days in a training with you.

You can put so much depth into this information, that it's really a no-brainer to say 'yes' to.

What I did with my Ultimate 48-Hour Author Program was exactly that. I knew I wanted people to have a book in their hands at the end of the experience.

On the table I included all the publishing, the editing, the first lot of 100 books, an ebook version, a Kindle upload, the transcription of their books, accommodation and all their meals.

It was quite a lot of expenses that I incurred and obviously I added my time that it would take to execute and deliver it for clients. I worked out what that would be.

Here is a sample of what our Table of Values looks like (overleaf).

Ultimate 48 Hour Author Retreats	Silver	Gold	Platinum
Mentoring & Accountability			
2 Hour Pre Weekend Prep Session One on One	✔	✔	✔
Unlimited Email Support	✔	✔	✔
Laser Mentoring until Book Release	✔	✔	✔
Ultimate 48 Hour Author Weekend Training & Support Including:	✔	✔	✔
1. Speaking Success System	✔	✔	✔
2. The Power of Social Media	✔	✔	✔
3. Connecting Through Video	✔	✔	✔
4. Free Publicity Generation	✔	✔	✔
5. Successful Publicity Follow Up System	✔	✔	✔
6. Pre-Launch Campaign	✔	✔	✔
7. Your Mindset Success	✔	✔	✔
Essentials for Success	✔	✔	✔
Luxury Accomodation	✔	✔	✔
Restaurant Style Meals	✔	✔	✔
Transcription of Your Book - 7 Hours Max		✔	✔
Webinar Set Up and Promotion to Explode Your Book Sales		✔	✔
Essential Checklist to Prepare You for the Weekend		✔	✔
Checklists/Guides up to Publishing Handover		✔	✔
Pre-Launch Campaign Set Up		✔	✔
Publishing		✔	✔
ISBN/Barcode		✔	✔
Copyediting (40 000 words max)		✔	✔
Internal Layout		✔	✔
Cover Creation (Including 3D Version)		✔	✔
100 Books (Black and White internal printing)		✔	✔
Author Photoshoot		✔	✔
E-Book Version of the Book		✔	✔
Library Deposit		✔	✔
Bonuses		✔	✔
Ultimate Product Generator Manual and Training Footage		✔	✔
Ninja Couch Marketing & Ultimate 48 Hour Author Books		✔	✔
Social Media Made Easy		✔	✔
Secrets to Running Webinars for Profit		✔	✔
12 Ninja Stars to Business Explosion E-Course (10 Hrs)		✔	✔
10 Easy Steps to Bust Your Money Limiting Beliefs		✔	✔
Ultimate Business Support Inner Circle Membership Lifetime		✔	✔
One on One Mentoring Support (3 Months)			✔

Email book@ultimate48hourauthor.com.au for a 30-minute Strategy Session to find out if you qualify to attend the weekend.

Follow Me Intensive 2 Day Workshop	Gold	VIP	Diamond
Mentoring & Accountability			
1 Hour Pre 2 Day Strategy Session One on One	x	x	x
Unimited Email Support (with Follow Me Team)	x	x	x
Laser Mentoring until your First Meetup (within 30 days from 2 Days)	x	x	x
Attendence to 2 Day Workshop including:			
Follow Me Manual	x	x	x
Follow Me copy of Paperback Book and Ebook	x	x	x
Follow Me Template Booklet	x	x	x
Starting Meetup Group at the 2 Day	x	x	x
Starting Facebook Group at the 2 Day	x	x	x
Follow Me USB with Templates	x	x	x
Dropbox with extra templates	x	x	x
Pre-Launch Campaign	x	x	x
Event Promotion and Bums on seats	x	x	x
Essentials For Success			
Meetup Mafia Facebook secret group and support	x	x	x
Webinar each month	x	x	x
Checklists before and after 2 days	x	x	x
Contracts and Templates	x	x	x
Coming up Monthly Meetup Mafia Meetup	x	x	x
Public Speaker Gigs around Australia with Meetup Mafia (subject to each Meetup Leader) choice			
Bonuses			
VA Program (teaching your assistant the Follow Me System)			
VA Program (we find you a Vistual assistant trained in the Follow Me System)			
One on One Exclusive Mentoring Support (3 months, 10 hours online)		x	
One on One Exclusive Mentoring Support at the Event and Face to Face (more then 10km from Bulimba QLD extra travelling fee of 20%)			x

Subject to current program at the time of your enquiry. Contact us at info@empoweringe

125

By application only! Contact: info@empoweringevents.com.au

Positioning Your High-End Programs

All I did was go out and tell people, 'Hey, these are the dates for my first retreat, this is what it's going to look like and this is what you'll get.' Until I sold it, I didn't start creating anything. The key here is that your high-end program never gets created until it's actually needed. It only gets positioned and itemised and then sold through the benefits of your lower-cost events.

If you only get a couple of people through in your first high-end program, it doesn't matter. You turn up for those people who want to be there for you. What amazing value if they receive a lot more of your attention and time. When we started doing our retreats we had a couple of smaller ones, which included 5 authors per retreat.

Since then we haven't had any less than 8, but we've had as many as 15 come along. I can tell you that obviously the smaller retreats get a lot more attention and a lot more of that one-on-one time. Never underestimate the size of the group or the experiences that they'll have with you. Always be willing to turn up for the people who want to commit to their success.

Tips for Your High-End Programs

1. Never create anything until you've sold it, because creating a high-end program will involve a lot more time. The key is to just pick your date of when it's going to be, because people like to operate with a timeline or a deadline. Work out the inclusions and obviously the structure of how you want to be paid. What works really well is to offer people some payment plans, but always ensure that your costs are covered before people come away, because you don't want to have cash flow issues. With us our program includes close to $10,000 worth of expenses. We have to collect that kind of sum before people come away on the retreat to ensure that we can also pay our suppliers, who are providing the different services through our package.

2. Filling it. Filling in these high-end programs, this is what everyone is curious about. How do you get people to invest so much with you? How do you get people there? It's through the funnel. We've talked a lot about running your own events, how to get people there and how to get speaking gigs, well it's the funnel that you create that takes clients through a sequence of steps that will get them into your high-end programs. Usually the best way is if you're doing a speaking gig, invite someone into your introductory event and from your introductory event they come into the high-end program.

It's very rare that people would come into your high-end program without having attended some kind of a face-to-face experience with you. Most of the time those people may be referrals from clients who you've already helped. You will get probably 10% of your high-end programs filled through word of mouth, some enquiries from people that have heard of you.

Others have vouched strongly for you; they have a lot of trust in you already. However, the 90% will come through people having physically met you. I have not yet met one entrepreneur that sells a program that's more than $10,000 that does not run face-to-face type of programs or events to meet the people that are going to ultimately do their high-end programs.

Once the person is in with you and has invested at least a few thousand dollars with you they generally like to stay within the community.

If you have future programs that are also at the high-end, then you're more likely to find it a lot easier that clients you've already had will return for another program to do another experience with you. It's because they already know what it's going to be like.

3. The last skill that you must master is actually selling it. How do you sell people into your program? A lot of people are scared of sales and selling. Who would invest thousands of dollars to spend this time with me? Have I got something to offer that's of value? There are those doubts that come up in our mind, when we haven't sold something at least once before. I always say, when you've sold your first one, you start to get that reference for success that you can sell more and that absolutely this is worthwhile. Someone's seeing the value in it and of course other people will see the value and the multiple times that you do sell it, your confidence and certainty in selling it becomes stronger and stronger.

What I recommend in this particular case is not to start out selling a high-end program. This is where I think a lot of people fail to monetise them or convert people. They try to sell off the stage. I think a program that's more than $3,000-$4,000 needs to be sold in a one-on-one conversation. What I would suggest for you to do is to invite people at the end of your speaking gigs, or hopefully at a longer event, like a half-day event or a full day event. You will prequalify them into your high-end program by having a one-on-one discussion to work out what their wants are, what their needs are and whether this is really a good fit for them. Then when you have that private time people don't feel that you're forcing them to step up and sign up in front of everyone else.

Always with high-end programs, in the selling process, have a couple of bonuses in your back pocket, that you can offer and add further value. Don't forget to put a limitation of when those bonuses expire. For instance: 'If you want to come along and join us on this high-end program, these are a couple of bonuses that I can offer you if you make a decision in the next 24-48 hours and pay your deposit. Then I'm happy to do that for you.'

That usually gives people that timeline, an awesome bonus that really almost doubles the value of the program, which means that if they're keen and they're ready to make their leap of faith experience (because this is what high-end programs are, for people it's a leap of faith). Usually, if they come back to you and say, 'Hey, I don't have the money. I'd like to do it but don't have the time.' It's either not a priority for them right now, or they're just scared of standing out, perhaps depending on what your program does. Time and money is always an excuse. They're actually not the core problem.

The Core Problem of the Hard Work

Usually the core problem is doubts over whether this will work for them, or whether they may not trust you enough or know you enough as yet. They might come back at a later stage. Another core reason could be along the lines of: 'Shit, if I sign into this transformational high-end program, I need to change.'

Sometimes that's actually very scary to the critter part of the brain in us. It might tell us, 'That means death for me! So in order to stay alive I won't go through with this.' Some people are scared that way because they know if they invest lots of money in a certain program there is something within us that pushes us to need to take that action and that is hard work.

I know for me in the past, time and money has come up as an excuse. Then I would actually ask myself the question, 'Hey, Natasa, what is this really about?' For me, I don't know about you, but for me it's always been about whether I'm willing to do the work. That's always been the core issue. Am I willing to do the work? Because if I commit to this, I bloody hell have to spend extra time away from my family to do things that make me feel uncomfortable; things that are really going to stretch me out of my comfort zone. So it's always been about whether I am willing to do the work.

That is the only question.

Certainly when we're talking about bums on seats in this particular book, am I willing to do the work? You know what guys? You have got work to do. Bums on seats is an art form as I've said and it takes effort and it takes some, as I like to call it, hustling and thinking of different ways who you need to reach out to. Who do I need to contact? Who do I need to collaborate with? Where do I need to post this? Where do I need to keep top of mind with people?

All of those things need to be considered and that is the thing that's going to lead people into filling your events, into selling your high-end programs and building that trust long-term. That takes work. If you're not willing to put in the work and the hours and doing 80% of promotional efforts and 20% of delivery and selling, then perhaps this is as far as you'll go as reading this book and going no further into this material.

Your numbers can be low in the early days, but turn up for those who commit to you, even if it's executing a high end program, it's worth it as generally your profit will be quite high on that; it's worthwhile turning up for anyone who wants to do it with you.

Table of Value Creation

In order to offer a high-end program, you need to show people what it includes and the different levels it has. Usually 3 options are the best. The table of value should include tangible items and intangible support or service based items.

Be creative with your niche around choosing tangibles. For example, when I did my weight loss niche I used to give people bathroom scales and a heart rate monitor watch. You can create books for people, but it doesn't have to be your book; it can be someone else's book that you think your client would highly benefit from. You can give them a sketchbook that can create a vision for their outcomes and their results. You can create many different things. Just think of the niche, think of what problem you're solving and what would be a really good complimentary product that you can give to them when they have that experience with you.

If you've never sold anything at such a high price point, start it with a price point where you're comfortable; where you know you'll be fairly rewarded for the work that you do. But you must believe the value; otherwise you'll not sell it. When I started my 48-Hour Author Program it was less than half the price where it is right now and that's where I was comfortable. Yes, there wasn't a huge profit margin, I did way too much work for what I was paid for and that is why we increased the price, because of the new system. Every time I increased it I notched it slightly up and every time I sold the first person into the next price point I had so much more confidence to go, 'Yeah, absolutely this is worth what it's worth.' Then I would subsequently sell others and they would come a lot easier.

Go out there and create that first table of value. Perhaps model one of the ones that we've got at the back of the book and that way you'll understand what it looks like and start showing it to people. Once the first person wants to buy it, then you've got a deadline.

131

Afterword

ow! You have made it through to the end of this life-changing book. Congratulations! We are truly humbled to have had you spend a few hours with us in creating and building a successful business via running public events. We want you to know that all of these strategies work and continue to so long as you are putting in the actions and effort to really make it happen.

Having successful events and lots of people wanting to attend takes time to build. Be kind to yourself, start small and build from there. We attracted smaller groups before we started getting the bigger numbers. At times we have stood in front of just one person, very small groups of 2-4 participants and travelled far to come home without a sale.

You must prove yourself and pay a price for success, you will have tests along this journey (they never stop even when you think you have reached a certain level of success). Say 'Yes' to every opportunity that comes your way, help people with their problems and come from a space of service and gratitude every single day.

We admire those who give something a red hot go, that commit and stick out the tougher early days. There is something to learn in every experience, with every person and in every situation. Take those learnings, adjust, pick yourself up and do it again.

Your shortcomings, perceived failures and setbacks make you a wiser business owner, event organiser and ultimately provide you with the best personal development journey you have ever had. Events are an amazing way to leverage your business and life to the next level. If you no longer want to sell your time for money and create experiences for your ideal clients, events are the way to go. If something isn't working do something else. If it is working, rinse and repeat, it's as simple as that.

We'd love to hear how you have gone with what we have been teaching you, so make sure you drop us a line via social media or via our contact details in this book. What was your favourite strategy, did you use one and amend it for yourself that is working wonders now? Tell us, we are on this learning curve also and are always looking for new, fresh ideas on how to get more *Bums on Seats*. See you in one of our event rooms soon.

Love Nat & Francesca xxx

About the Authors

Natasa Denman

Natasa Denman was born and raised in Skopje, Macedonia up to the age of 14 after which she immigrated to Melbourne, Australia with her mum. She didn't speak English and found it challenging in the first two years to fit into the new country and culture. Her zest for learning and achievement fast tracked this process and she had high performance results in her academic endeavours.

Natasa has a Bachelor of Applied Science (Psychology/Psychophysiology), Diploma in Life Coaching, NLP Practitioner Certification, Practitioner of Matrix Therapies, holds a Black Belt in Taekwondo and is a Professional Certified Coach (PCC) through the International Coaching Federation.

She started her business in May 2010 and after a very slow first year she decided to write her first book *The 7 Ultimate Secrets to Weight Loss*, which was released in June 2011. This book put her

first business on the map and enabled her husband to join her full time in the business a year later. She is a contributor of *You Can ... Live the Life of Your Dreams* and a co-author of *Ninja Couch Marketing*, author of *Ultimate 48 Hour Author*, contributor in *Successfully Speaking* and author of *Natasa Denman Reveals... 1000 Days to a Million Dollar Coaching Business from Home.*

The last three years, she has successfully built up Ultimate 48 Hour Author to a 7-figure business from home. She travels all around Australia to speak, run events and workshops, which is how she is able to run her signature retreats – Ultimate 48 Hour Author. To date she has successfully completed 10 retreats and helped over 100 people become first time authors. Her passion and enthusiasm for her program is what people love. Her authors come from all over the country and internationally to be part of this end-to-end program. She prides herself with the 100% success rate that is achieved via this program.

In her six years in business, Natasa has run hundreds of webinars, over 100 public events, hosted over 50 Networking Meetups, spoken at over 200 other events and completed 10 high-end retreats. *Bums on Seats* was something her clients always struggle with and this was the book to bring those strategies and secrets to the forefront.

Natasa is a mum of three, Judd 7, Mika 5 and Xara 18 months. She loves living her Ultimate Lifestyle whilst helping others do the same through the systems, programs and consulting she provides. Natasa was the Ausmumpreneur Finalist for Product Innovation in 2014.

Natasa's Contact Details:
Web: www.natasadenman.com
Web: www.ultimate48hourauthor.com.au
Email: natasa@natasadenman.com

Francesca Moi

F rancesca Moi was born in Sardinia and raised in Faenza, Italy up to the age of nineteen. She then moved to London, Madrid, Valencia and Rhodos and Kos Islands before finally immigrating to Australia on her own in 2008. She didn't speak English very well and found it challenging in the first few years to fit into a new country and culture. Her zest for learning and achievement fast-tracked this process and she obtained good results in her studies.

Francesca has a certificate in Neuro Linguistic Programming, Hypnosis, Time-based Technique, Neuro Relationship Technique, Reiki Practitioner and a doctorate degree at Mind Mechanix.

Being creative and running workshops and events for business owners was something she never planned to do. Her passion for business and marketing was the reason she started her second Meetup in December 2014, the Entrepreneurs' Abundance Mindset group. She is now a motivated entrepreneur who has a passion for communities and marketing with over 12,000 followers over various social medias.

Francesca just recently published her very first book, *Follow Me: ShutttUppp and Build your Network*, also with the help of her friend/colleague/author Natasa Denman. The book, which has been pre-selling since November 2015 had already sold over a hundred copies Australia wide.

> **Francesca's Contact Details**
> **Web**: www.empoweringevents.com.au
> **Web**: www.francescamoi.com/followme
> **Email**: francescamoi@empoweringevents.com.au

Appendices

Checklist 1: 14 days to event

Item	Done ☑	Notes
Plan Your Year (Start from your BIG Offer + Smaller offer + Book Meetup Dates)	☐	
Book Venues for the whole year (Book Projector + Flip Chart)	☐	
Pick Guest Speakers and book them in	☐	
Buy Pens + Note Pads for Marketing	☐	
Schedule first Meetup + Hot Description + Photos on meetup.com (first 5 free)	☐	
Always put a limit in the guest allowed on the night so that you create scarcity	☐	
Create a Facebook event + invite friends	☐	
Door Prize (make sure you have a door prize if not ask the attendees to organize some)	☐	
Make sure you keep an eye on numbers of tickets	☐	
Share Meetup group everywhere (on facebook groups + profile + meetup mafia)	☐	

Checklist 2: 10 days to event		
Item	**Done ☑**	**Notes**
Keep checking tickets availability	☐	
Send an email out – 10 days to go!! (with new announcement – venue or Guest Speaker + ticket realised)	☐	
Keep adding tickets	☐	
Reply to all comments on Meetup and Facebook	☐	
Do a Video Periscope talking about a sneak peek TIP that you will also share at the Meetup and invite people to join you	☐	
PROMOTE PROMOTE PROMOTE	☐	

Checklist 3: 3 days to event		
Item	**Done ☑**	**Notes**
Keep checking tickets availability	☐	
Send an email out – 3 days to go!! (with new announcement – Get them excited + ticket realised + let them know how many people booked)	☐	
Keep adding tickets	☐	
Reply to all comments on Meetup and Facebook	☐	
Do a Video Periscope talking about a sneak peek TIP that you will also share at the Meetup and invite people to join you	☐	
PROMOTE PROMOTE PROMOTE	☐	

Checklist 4: 1 day to event		
Item	**Done ☑**	**Notes**
Keep checking tickets availability	☐	
Send an email out – 1 day to go with info about parking and address and time + link to book!!	☐	
Keep adding tickets until 30 min before (don't give up!)	☐	
Reply to all comments on Meetup and Facebook	☐	
Do a Video Periscope talking about a sneak peek TIP that you will also share at the Meetup and invite people to join you	☐	
PROMOTE PROMOTE PROMOTE	☐	

Checklist 5: The day of the event

Item	Done ☑	Notes
Keep checking tickets availability	☐	
Send an email out – 1 day to go with info about parking and address and time + link to book!!	☐	
Keep adding tickets until 30 min before (don't give up!)	☐	
Reply to all comments on Meetup and Facebook (on the day there usually are lots of questions)	☐	
Prepare Registration Forms (with your logo)	☐	
Name Tags and Spare Blank Tags	☐	
Handouts or Flyers	☐	
Pens, Textas and Paper for Note Taking	☐	
Laptop and Charger	☐	
Projector and Power Cord	☐	

Projector Stand and Presenter Pointer	☐	
Feedback Forms	☐	
Product	☐	
Door Prizes	☐	
Music, Speakers, Charger	☐	
Run Sheet	☐	
Suitcase to Carry Everything	☐	
Video Camera, Tripod & Charger	☐	
Extension Cable + projector attachments	☐	
Irresistible Offer Sign up Sheets (in case people ask)	☐	
Release Form for Videoing Event	☐	
Phone and Charger	☐	

Release Form

Date: __ __ . __ __ . __ __ __ __

By signing this form I give permission to [YOUR NAME] to take photos and videos during this workshop.

I understand that I am not paid for these photos, and that [YOUR NAME] will only use these photos in a positive light for marketing purposes.

Name	Signature

Workshop Feedback Form

"Event Name"

Date: __ __ . __ __ . __ __ __ __

Presenter: _____

How would you rate the following (please check and mark in the appropriate column)?

Poor	Fair	Average	Good	Excellent
1	2	3	4	5

	1	2	3	4	5
1. Value of the workshop meeting your needs					
2. Expertise of the presenter					
3. Presentation techniques of the presenter					
4. Your learning experience					
5. Clarity of objectives					
6. Active involvement of the participants in the learning experience.					
7. Timeliness of the material presented					
8. Use of practical examples					
9. Level of interest in the presented topics					
10. Overall rating of the session					

What guidance could you give the presenter to improve this learning experience?

What did you learn today that you are most likely to try?

Who in your world do you know that you would love to give the GIFT of attending this workshop in the future?

Name: _____

Email: _____ **Mob:** _____

Name: _____

Email: _____ **Mob:** _____

Name: _____

Email: _____ **Mob:** _____

Name: _____

Email: _____ **Mob:** _____

Work with Natasa & Francesca

Bums on Seats Online Course

*A*re you ready to double if not triple your strategies in getting Bums on Seats? Natasa and Francesca came together for one full day of filming (over 13 hours in lockdown) to bring you additional value for your Events Success.

In over 7 Hours of Online training, you will be taken through each of the 12 stages with further tips, tools and strategies to move your forward in your journey.

This is your opportunity to get up close and personal with Natasa & Francesca. Their bubbly personalities will keep you engaged for hours! The key is to take action as you are learning. Set up your events and follow the steps – it's the only way to embed the learning.

The Course has been divided into 12 x 30 Minute Lessons so that you can take the recommended actions between each one.

Available to purchase here:

www.bumsonseats.net.au

As Speakers ...

EE

EMPOWERING EVENTS

FRANCESCA MOI

Starting fresh as an Entrepreneur in Australia, Francesca realised that the power lies in your Network.

With no friends or family in Australia Francesca decided to grow her community and she did that using 'MeetUp' and Facebook.

Francesca create a system to show her clients how to build a profitable Network of raving fans.

From 0 Members to over 10000 people in her meetups in only a few months Francesca has generated a 6 figure Business for herself and for her client's via workshops and training programs. She was soon nominated "the MeetUp Queen".

Francesca is the Published Author of the book "Follow Me – Shutuppp and Build your Network!"

ancesca is available for Speaking
igs and can present about:

How to Profitably Network
How could you leverage from Meetup
and Faceboook groups
How to 'Sell without Selling'
Mindset
How to create a Powerful Following
Leadership

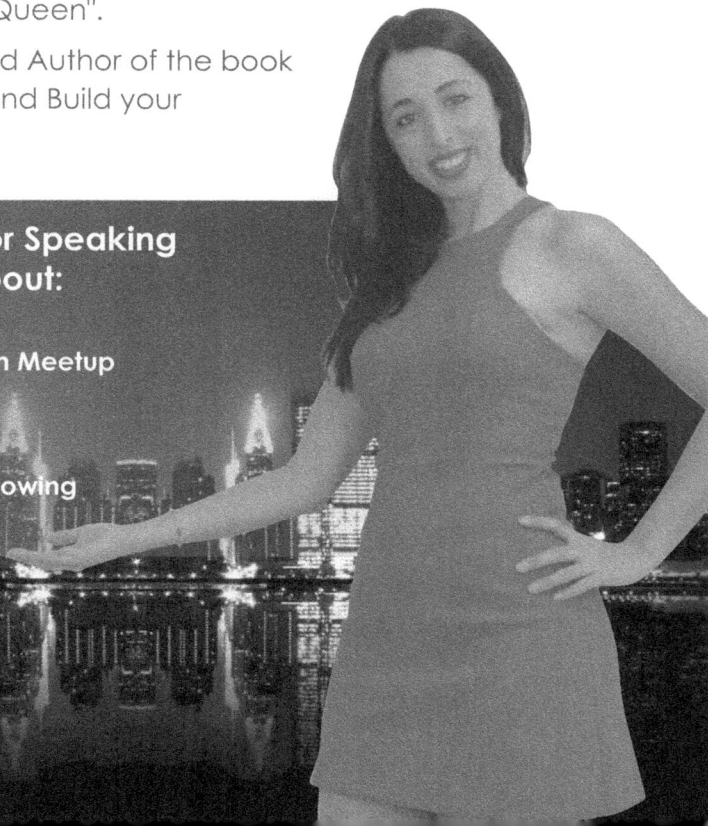

YAY PSA 2016!

FUTURE AUTHORS!

SYDNEY FULL HOUSE

NATASA SMASHED IT!
Thank you Inspiring Entrepreneurs, YOU ROCK!

NEXT EVENT
WED 9th March: BEN ANGEL
GET YOUR TICKETS HERE:
bit.ly/BrandingForEntrepreneurs-Melb

Meetup

#BrandMeMelb

EMPOWERING EVENTS

by Francesca Moi

BUMS ON SEATS